HOTEL CHIC at HOME

HOTEL CHIC at HOME

INSPIRED DESIGN
IDEAS FROM
GLAMOROUS
ESCAPES

SARA BLISS

The Monacelli Press

Contents

Preface

For decades, travelers had limited choices of places to spend the night. There were cookie-cutter chains washed in beige, covered in stain-resistant fabrics, and designed to be bland enough to not turn anyone off. Or lovely, incredibly formal, grand hotels steeped in history, antiques, and awash in marble. On a smaller scale, the B & B country inn became a trend in the 1970s and 1980s, with floral everything—wallpaper, bedspreads, curtains. When boutique hotels burst on the scene in the late 1980s and early 1990s, the hotel world was totally transformed.

There are debates as to which hotel started the craze, but Manhattan's Morgans Hotel was definitely one of the first; it opened in 1984. Started by Studio 54 founders Steve Rubell and Ian Schrager, the hotel was a fluid next step. Downstairs was a buzzy restaurant and bar where even locals wanted to hang out. Upstairs were gorgeous interiors by designer Andrée Putman, with photos by Robert Mapplethorpe in the guest rooms. It was cool, glamorous, and a place to be seen.

Rubell and Schrager followed the success with the equally chic Royalton in 1988. Clean, sparse, all-white interiors designed by Philippe Starck gave the hotel a completely fresh look. The industry quickly picked up on the fact that the design of a hotel could suddenly become one of its strongest assets. Hoteliers began using design to create truly one-of-a-kind environments, ones that often reflected the hip style of the city outside. After decades of copycat hotel rooms, where rooms looked the same in Tokyo as in Toledo, the unique hotel concept was here to stay. The Hôtel Costes in Paris opened to rave reviews in 1991 with a dramatic design by Jacques Garcia. The Delano hit Miami in 1994, taking a former Art Deco property and making it feel new again thanks to an infusion of white furniture and Starck's cheeky take on design. When the W Hotel followed in 1998 in Manhattan, it proved that the boutique hotel concept could work for a chain; so long as each successive W created its own look.

The explosion of boutique hotels continues, with ever-more-creative ideas for design being embraced. Hotel owners have partnered with some of the best designers in the world, including Michele Bonan, Ilse Crawford, Kit Kemp, India Mahdavi, Roman and Williams, and Kelly Wearstler. Hotel clients seem to be willing to push design to the extremes—whether that means using cutting-edge furniture, bold color, standout pattern, or new twists on traditional craftsmanship. The most dynamic, innovative, and exciting rooms are coming out of hotels, not private residences.

The best hotel designs can utterly transport you. Want to feel glamorous? Check into Francis Ford Coppola's Palazzo Margherita in Bernalda, Italy, where even the bathrooms feature hand-painted frescoes on the soaring ceilings, and brightly colored, zigzag mosaic tile floors bring the sixteenth-century palace firmly into the present. Want to feel like part of the indie music scene? Stay at the Ace Portland, where vintage band posters line the walls and every room comes with classic LPs and a turntable. If you want to feel like a part of today's jet set, check into the J.K. Place Capri, a mansion overlooking the sea that's designed to feel like the home of an incredibly sophisticated friend. Or if life feels too hectic, and you need complete serenity and Zen, no clutter or color in sight, Aman Resorts are your go-to brand.

That powerfully transformative effect of travel often leads to that moment on vacation when we think, "Why can't my life be more like this every day?" That's really the idea behind *Hotel Chic at Home*—inspiring readers to re-create the coolest aspects of hotel life in real life. Maybe it's filling your home with the African pop music you heard in Kenya. Perhaps it's cooking the recipe for that anniversary dinner you had in France—back home in Florida. Or maybe it's covering your headboard in a Moroccan textile simply to make everyday life feel a bit more exotic.

Hotels are wonderful places to look not only for great design ideas, but for real-life design solutions. Even the chicest hotels have the same issues as most homeowners—awkward spaces, cookie-cutter architecture, lackluster views, or dark rooms. The difference is that hoteliers have figured out how to use design to solve those dilemmas—after all, they have to book every room, every night.

In these pages you will find clever ideas that offer real answers for our own homes. The hundreds of images from the most innovative boutique hotels around the world show how to maximize a teeny room with a smart furniture layout; how to enhance a dark space with pattern, color, and lighting; or how to jazz up bland architecture with unique details. Wish you had a library full of classic books and first editions but really you have cheap paperbacks and a Kindle? Put up library wallpaper like The Pig Hotel in the Cotswolds. The paper, which features a faux bookshelf lined with classics, is so real guests often try to grab the spines. Looking to break out of the all-white bathroom rut? Check out the zig-zag tile wall—a wow effect created simply by clever placement of green and white subway tiles. Want a large space to feel instantly warmer? Use fabric to cover walls rather than wallpaper, like they do at the Haymarket Hotel in London—there's nothing cozier. Not sure what to do with a wing chair that has been passed down from your grandparents? Add fringe like designer India Mahdavi did at The Connaught for an instant update.

Whether you are looking to bring the spirit of Marrakech back to your pad in Minneapolis or simply want to use the dark and dramatic interiors of the C.O.Q. in Paris to transform an all-white condo, there are hundreds of ideas here to get you started. My hope is that you will be able to use this volume in many ways—as a design bible, as inspiration for your personal travel bucket list, or even just to escape for a few minutes without leaving your couch.

BEDROOMS

An Ode to Dark Bedrooms

Too many hotels feature layouts that are boxy, similar, and uninspired. Art? Purchased in multiples. Bedding? White. Wall color? Cream or beige. You really could be anywhere in the world—not to mention anywhere in the hotel itself—since there are usually hundreds of rooms, all exactly alike. Certain chain hotels only offer bedrooms that look as though they could equally be in Dallas or Dubai. It's the opposite of how a bedroom is supposed to feel, which of course is intensely personal and private. The best bedrooms feel like reflections of their owners' interests, styles, and passions with unique takes on art, color, pattern, and furniture.

Thankfully, many hotels now design their guest rooms to feel more the way a bedroom at home would: comfortable, intriguing, and one-of-a-kind. When you stay in one of these rooms, you are made to feel like it's the only place on the globe where you would be having that particular experience. Parisian and Moroccan hotels are particularly adept at

creating mood and spectacular spaces, likely because those two destinations have a history of celebrating design. The Hotel Providence in Paris is a perfect example: Elodie Moussié, wife of the restaurateur Pierre Moussié, designed the interiors of the former brothel that dates to 1854 with her best friend, Sophie Richard. Walls in leafy prints or inky hues, paired with one-of-a-kind vintage furniture like starburst headboards and nineteenth-century bars, combine to reimagine these classic rooms into sexy, sophisticated, and inspired spaces.

Ideally, your bedroom should be a place where you escape from the stresses of the world—a haven where you feel ready to unwind and recharge, regardless of what is happening beyond its walls. For some, achieving that via design means being surrounded by florals; for others it means soothing, pale hues; and for a few it means painting walls a transporting dark shade.

Dark wall colors are not for the faint of heart. This power decorating tactic will outshine everything and anything else in the space. For that reason, it works well with minimal or very basic furniture silhouettes. For example, at the C.O.Q. Hotel in Paris, beds have no headboards and a simple desk and chair are the only other furniture in the room; one vintage portrait—scored at a flea market—is the only art in each room. Imagine that same space in white. It just wouldn't be memorable. Painted in a hybrid of dark green, navy, and gray, however, the room is spectacular. Sometimes paint is all you need to make a real impact.

PREVIOUS PAGES: Deep wall colors work best in rooms that are at either end of the spectrum in terms of natural light: very bright or very dark. This corner room at the Hotel Providence in Paris, for example, is bathed in sunlight; the inky-blue, almost-black shade looks stunning with the unexpected contrast.

ABOVE LEFT: A guest room at Ett Hem in Stockholm, designed by Ilse Crawford, captures the feeling that you're staying in the home of someone very intriguing. The spaces are filled with an unexpected combination of details, including the unusual gray-green walls, sculptural rattan chair, mirrored sideboard, and ornate chandelier.

ABOVE: Green is an infamously tricky color to get right; this rich, leafy shade strikes a perfect balance between colorful and cool at the Greenwich Hotel in New York. Adding varying shades of green throughout the space underscores the boldness and deliberateness of the choice. The balcony doors are deep forest green, the shantung curtains are a muted pale green, and a vintage armchair is recovered in sage green velvet.

ABOVE: The C.O.Q. Hotel in Paris is proof that all you really need to make a statement in a bedroom is a dark, seductive hue like this breathtaking deep blue-green shade. In fact, the wall color is the space's only real design flourish—there's no headboard on the bed and the furniture is simple.

BELOW: If complete commitment to a strong wall color seems daunting, an unexpected way to temper it is by using it only on part of the wall. At The Hoxton in Amsterdam, designed by Nicemakers, colorblocked navy functions as virtual wainscoting, keeping the space from feeling too dark and adding a graphic punch to the room.

OPPOSITE: When choosing colors for small spaces, opt for hues that complement each other, even if they are separated by a wall or partition. At the Vidago Palace in Portugal, the deep-blue living space makes the beige room's exceptional, contemporary, cherry-blossom design pop.

OPPOSITE: Sometimes the best way to solve a "problem" with a small space is to call attention to it. A dark blanket and bolster on a small platform bed transform a teeny nook at the Ace Hotel in Portland, Oregon, into a memorable bedroom. Salvaged planks line the back wall, framing and defining the space's rustic mood.

THIS PAGE, TOP: In a move that proves how cool eco-friendly design can be, AvroKO featured reclaimed redwood from New York City water tanks on guest room walls at 1 Hotel Central Park. The design choice makes the room feel cozy and incorporates a tactile element. It also reinforces a connection to the architectural history of the city.

THIS PAGE, CENTER: Certain woods evoke a certain association. At The Cape in Los Cabos, Mexico, wide, dark wood boards stretched along one wall immediately create a tropical vibe that adds texture to the room while creating a contrast to the blue ocean expanses beyond.

THIS PAGE, BOTTOM: Design staples associated with effortlessly hip style—wood-plank-lined walls, antlers, and plaid—are all captured in this Palihotel Melrose guest room. The cool and quirky log-cabin look could work as well in Louisiana as it does in Los Angeles.

Transforming Textiles

Fabric is second only to paint in its ability to immediately refresh a room or to make it memorable. Design-centered hotels around the world recognize this and have come up with an amazing array of ways to use fabric to give a space character. From Suzanis to sheepskins, the many innovative ways different materials, prints, details, patterns, and color ranges are used is inspiring. Surrounding a space with wonderfully tactile materials creates an alluring environment that is key in a bedroom. Hotels also carefully consider the atmosphere they want to evoke: if it's quiet calm, vast expanses of cream cotton might do the trick; for visual excitement, it might be textiles from Belize.

Many of the most memorable hotel rooms use fabric to transform a space in astonishing ways. One of the simplest ways of adding dimension and interest to a room is by creating a small canopy, just with fabric—no bedframe required. The Hotel Recamier incorporated 1930s-inspired prints into its rooms to create neat, precise, and graphic baldachins above each bed. A mirror layered right on top of the fabric and above the headboard completes the simple, chic look. Owner Sylvie de Lattre and designer Jean-Louis Deniot incorporated 1930s-inspired prints into the rooms at the Hotel Recamier to create neat, precise, and graphic baldachins above each bed. A white square canopy hung from a very high ceiling at the Dar Seven in Marrakech creates a breathtakingly romantic room while drawing attention to the bed—and away from the room's narrow proportions.

These chic canopies can be recreated by sewing together two contrasting fabrics—one print on either side and rod pockets at the "joints." Add two rods and two ceiling-mounted brackets and voilà. The fabrics in the Hotel Recamier's rooms are all custom reeditions of 1930s and 1940s motifs from famed French textile manufacturer Le Manach, but similarly scaled prints or vintage fabrics would work just as beautifully.

LEFT: The owner and designer of the Jnane Tamsna, Marrakech, Meryanne Loum-Martin, draped a graphic Suzani textile over the bed, increasing its length by sewing white fabric on either side. A red blanket and two red carpets placed on either side of the bed highlight the fabric's bold hues.

OPPOSITE, TOP: Accentuating one unexpected element gives a room verve. This red-quilted headboard at El Fenn in Marrakech rises all the way to the ceiling. In this case, the visual line distracts from the room's narrow proportions; the same trick will make any room's ceilings look higher.

OPPOSITE, BELOW: At the Jnane Tamsna, one guest room creates drama in two ways with just fabric. White canvas the same width as the bed features a band of striped pattern—an Uzbek ikat stitched in the center. It is a clever way to incorporate any interesting fabric, from a Batik to an Indian block-printed textile. Curtains with inset stripes reinforce the motif.

LEFT: In this suite at Francis Ford Coppola's Blancaneaux Lodge in Belize, local textiles are used as pillows, throws, and even hung as art.

ABOVE: Designer Martyn Lawrence Bullard makes an impression with different outsized Suzanis in each room at the Colony Palms Hotel in Palm Springs, most notably as headboards. The ancient textile art features vibrant colors and graphic patterns.

BELOW: Local meets global at New York City's Ludlow Hotel. The guest rooms feature Moroccan pendant lamps, Indo-Portuguese-style beds, and petrified wood nightstands from Organic Modernism in Brooklyn, as well as curtains that feature a contemporary take on marbling and sheepskin-covered side chairs.

PREVIOUS PAGES: To make a wood paneled room at Chalet Pelerin in the French Alps feel warm and alluring, No. 12 Interiors incorporated sumptuous fabrics like sheepskin, cashmere, and wool in shades that echo the room's natural materials.

THIS PAGE, CLOCKWISE FROM TOP LEFT: The designers for Nayara Springs in Costa Rica, the Nihiwatu in Indonesia, the Pousada Picinguaba in Brazil, the Four Seasons on Koh Samui in Thailand, and the Singita Sasakwa in South Africa may be separated by continents, but they all recognize that nothing evokes a tropical escape like a bed draped with a veil of transparent white fabric.

The Power of Pattern

Prints and patterns are powerful design tools. A great print can distract from a room's flaws—lack of light, odd proportions, or low ceilings. An eye-catching fabric can make a tired piece of furniture instantly look new again. If your windows are lacking a view, drawing the eye toward vibrantly patterned curtains is a way to compensate. For example, at c/o The Maidstone in East Hampton and the Saint James in Paris, wallpaper with vertical lines makes rooms with low ceilings appear higher. A wallpaper with a bold, overscaled motif and a dark background, as is used at the Captain Fairfield in Maine, can conversely make a large room feel cozier or distract from a dark space. To make a room appear bigger, choose a print with a white background like the designers did at the Palihouse in Santa Monica, California.

Pattern that evokes the outdoors has the power to transport, which can be particularly magical in a bedroom. Want to connect with nature even in the middle of a city? Try the verdant House of Hackney Palmeral wallpaper, which brings a jungle-chic Art Deco sensibility into a teeny bedroom at the Hotel Providence in Paris. If you want to be surrounded by blooms all year round, take a cue from the Lowell Hotel in New York. There, a de Gournay paper inspired by eighteenth-century Chinese motifs covers walls with branches, flowers, and birds for a room that feels like never-ending spring.

ABOVE: This black-and-white wallpaper's M.C. Escher-esque print works as an optical illusion in its own right. Its vertical repeat makes the viewer forget how small this guest room at the Saint James in Paris really is.

RIGHT: Designer Kit Kemp is known for skillfully mixing color and pattern. In this bedroom at the Ham Yard Hotel in London, gray fabric-covered walls set a neutral backdrop for dazzling prints. Kemp's own Tulu fabric for Chelsea Textiles covers the headboard while her pink Moondog print is featured on the pillows.

OVERLEAF: Proving you can never have too many patterns, this suite at the c. 1892 Palazzo Margherita in Bernalda, Italy, features Italian tile zigzag floors, a North African–inspired headboard, and an inlay chest. Recently restored by hotelier and filmmaker Francis Ford Coppola and designer Jacques Grange, guests wake up to beautifully restored paintings and frescos on walls and ceilings.

LEFT: The House of Hackney's Palmeral wallpaper brings a leafy, tropical spirit to the Hotel Providence in Paris. A deep-green blanket mirrors the wallpaper's rich hue.

OPPOSITE, TOP: The next best thing to waking up in a garden would be starting the day in the enchanting Garden Suite at the Lowell Hotel in Manhattan. Interior designer Michael S. Smith covered the bedroom walls with a print by de Gournay inspired by eighteenth-century Chinese motifs.

OPPOSITE, BOTTOM: The vertical lines in a mustard-yellow-and-gray wallpaper pattern help give the illusion of higher ceilings in a top-floor guest room at c/o The Maidstone in East Hampton, New York. The paper is from Casamance.

OPPOSITE, TOP: The design of all of the Palihouse hotels trends funky and personal. Details like the quirky Abnormals Anonymous Sea Tales wallpaper featuring seaweed trees and squid give the Santa Monica hotel its unique charm and do more for the room than any traditional toile ever could.

OPPOSITE, BOTTOM: When one large rug in a contemporary color but traditional design is used as a statement in an otherwise simple space, it reads as a strong pattern as well, as it does here at the Palihouse in West Hollywood.

RIGHT: Designer Annsley McAleer skillfully mixed patterns and prints at The Christopher on Martha's Vineyard. Though Quadrille's Persia wallpaper features an intricate pattern, rendered in gray and white it reads as a neutral backdrop. Vibrant orange and blue Stella fabric from Tulu Textiles on the headboard dictates the rest of the bedroom's color scheme. Other accessories in blue include Nina Farmer Interiors pillows and Safavieh's Color Swirls glass table lamp.

The Benefits of All-White Spaces

White rooms are like vanilla ice cream: a lovely choice in and of itself that often gets overshadowed by more creative flavors. There are lots of benefits to white, however. The color is a perpetual favorite for its ability to create the feeling of a more expansive space. In the diminutively sized guest rooms at the Marlton Hotel in New York—some are only 125 square feet—a crisp backdrop keeps the space from feeling claustrophobic. Contemporary black lighting and intricate moldings keep the room intriguing and chic without overwhelming the tiny space.

When everything in a room is rendered in white or ivory, the walls seem to recede even more, making it a smart design choice for small spaces. Keeping not just one, but a variety of rooms in an all-white palette will link the spaces and make the entire home look larger. To get a sense of what this would look like, check out the guest rooms at the Viceroy Sugar Beach on St. Lucia. The key pieces—the bed, desk, bench, and side tables—feature classic lines and share the same ivory shade. This creates an airy, open feeling. It's also a good color choice when you have gorgeous views outdoors. Nature's vibrant greenery and seascapes will look that much more lovely when looking out from a white room.

Another benefit to white walls is that they tend to spotlight furniture. They allow intrinsically intriguing pieces, such as an antique headboard or a modern four-poster bed, to truly stand out. So it's not a surprise that architects and design junkies often gravitate toward one of the innumerable colors available in the white spectrum as the backdrop for contemporary or modern furniture that has bold lines.

Pure, monochromatic ivory floods a cottage at the Viceroy Sugar Beach in St. Lucia, keeping the feeling at once tropical and crisply tailored.

LEFT: This design trick from the Viceroy Santa Monica offers an intriguing alternative to the standard headboard. A symmetrical arrangement of square and rectangular mirrors creates a showstopping backdrop for a bed. It adds reflected color without introducing a new hue, keeping the palette simple but interesting.

BELOW: Designer Sean MacPherson was inspired by Parisian hotels when he revamped the Marlton Hotel in Manhattan. Quintessentially French details such as boiserie, reproduction beds in classic French antique shapes, and brass sconces add up to a pretty, serene space—which is then turned on its head by a Serge Mouille ceiling lamp that offers an unexpected, modern design twist.

OPPOSITE: A grouping of four hand-painted tiles doubles as art in this bedroom at Casas del XVI in the Dominican Republic.

OVERLEAF: One oversize piece of art or photography can create all the memorable impact a room needs, especially if it's otherwise furnished with Spartan white linens and minimal furniture, as with the Grace Mykonos, in Greece.

Power Colors

There was a time when I painted everything a different shade of light blue. My bedroom? Very pale, cloudy sky blue. My living room? A deeper shade that looked fun paired with a red couch and curtains. My son's room? Teal. Something about blue felt beachy and relaxed, and I wanted that vibe despite being in New York City. However, eventually it started to feel like a safe—and completely boring—choice. I wanted to go bolder, and I found inspiration in hotels. I'll admit that my living room is now navy, which I acknowledge is still blue, but the rich color was inspired by the glamorous living space at the J.K. Place Capri. For my bedroom, I took note of the deep gray/green hue at the C.O.Q. in Paris and copied the dark shade—I swear I sleep better in that astonishing color.

So many forward-thinking designers are experimenting with color in fresh ways. At The Merchant in Salem, Massachusetts, it's impossible not to be impressed by designer Rachel Reider's deft combination of a circular brown wallpaper, an abstract black-and-white headboard fabric, green curtains, green leopard-print pillows, a purple throw, and black trim on the walls and ceiling. Even if you just extracted a few elements of the room to re-create—brown, purple, and kelly green—it's still a sophisticated and unusual spin on a color palette. Looking to hotels for different color ideas will always yield some unexpected palettes—whether it's the glamorous pairing of bright green and gold at Casa Fayette, in Guadalajara, Mexico, or the soothing shades of pale pink and gray at The Chequit on Shelter Island.

OPPOSITE: To give a room filled with different prints a sophisticated edge and a unifying element, paint the doors and trim a glossy black. It's a design trick that works beautifully in this guest room at The Merchant in Salem, Massachusetts.

ABOVE: Geometric pattern La Fiorentina by design legend David Hicks never gets old. The pink-and-wine, diamond-print curtains command the room at the Captain Fairfield Inn in Kennebunkport, Maine.

LEFT: Pops of green in riffs on different classic patterns enliven the neutral, grasscloth-covered walls of a suite at The Merchant.

OPPOSITE, TOP: The rooms at The Chequit Hotel show how effective colorblocking can be. If designer and owner Kevin O'Shea had painted the guest rooms all gray, they would have appeared too severe; entirely in pink, they would have felt too girly. Paired together, however, they play off each other in a fresh and sophisticated way.

OPPOSITE, BOTTOM: A heavily lacquered, green headboard with a built-in, gold-painted shelf combines a contemporary profile with glamorous color at Casa Fayette in Guadalajara, Mexico.

Statement Beds

All it takes is one gorgeous piece to transform any space. In a bedroom, going with a showstopping bed is sometimes all you need to make a statement. Think about the prevailing mood you want to create in a room, then design the bed to reflect it. Do you want a more rustic sensibility? Choose a birch poster bed like those at the Ranch at Rock Creek in Montana. Are you going for a romantic look? Find a wrought-iron canopy bed with beautiful lines like the one at Dar Seven in Morocco.

One of the biggest factors in determining what style the bed evokes is the material. A bed crafted out of teak or mahogany gives off a strong, solid sensibility, while a canopy bed draped in yards of chiffon or cotton exudes a more romantic, soft energy. The unique mahogany poster bed at Edson Hill in Stowe, Vermont, and the canopy bed at Dar

Seven, in Marrakech, created from yards of billowing white fabric, are a case in point. The bed at Dar Seven is all the more showstopping due to the height, and instantly creates a dreamy environment by surrounding its guest in white. At Edson Hill, the dark wood feels masculine while the spooled

---

PREVIOUS PAGES, LEFT: Rustic meets refined in a guest room at the Wild Rabbit in the English Cotswolds. The pale stone room features a handmade chestnut bed that pairs with a flax-colored, upholstered headboard to create a study in modulated natural tones.

PREVIOUS PAGES, RIGHT: A contemporary take on the canopy bed boasts a striking shape in an innovative material: copper. The eye-catching piece was designed by Ilaria Miani, who also was the visionary behind the interiors at this Tuscan hotel, Monteverdi,

silhouette creates a geometric detail that's both tactile and intriguing. Both beds dictate the mood of these hotel rooms in a profound way.

Thanks to small spaces and the desire to make a lasting impact, many hotel designers understand the power of a sculptural bed. Take the copper canopy bed at Monteverdi in Italy. Against beige walls in a space with minimal furniture, the canopy frame forms graphic lines and shapes that make it look like a work of art. The fun, of course, is that while the bed is aesthetically very cool, it's also practical, providing an amazing place to rest your head at the end of the day.

OPPOSITE, ABOVE: This black birch bed at the Ranch at Rock Creek in Montana captures the rustic, outdoorsy spirit of the West. The strong lines are enhanced with contrasting white bedding and sheer white fabric wrapped around the posts.

OPPOSITE, BOTTOM: Balinese woodwork is highlighted throughout the serene retreat Amankila, in Bali. The muted palette and single wood tone makes the space feel soothing. Choosing a bed frame carved from a tropical wood and featuring an exotic motif will immediately lend a global note to any bedroom.

ABOVE: At Dar Seven in Marrakech, an unadorned, wrought-iron canopy bed's romantic lines are highlighted against all-white walls. Intricate window grills and interior shutters add to the romantic sensibility.

LEFT: Draping yards of fabric from a concealed ceiling frame could create a similar look as this bedroom at Dar Seven in Marrakech. Owner Princess Letizia Ruspoli and designer Jérôme Vermelin used the white canopy to evoke drama and romance.

OPPOSITE, TOP: At Vermont's Edson Hill, a mahogany bed with intricately turned posters from Noir updates the antique style. Choosing a white backdrop highlights the bed's sculptural lines and makes it the centerpiece of the room.

OPPOSITE, BOTTOM: The sturdy profile of this headboard commands the room at Casas del XVI in the Dominican Republic; a similar piece would create a Spanish Colonial feeling anywhere.

Designing the Ceiling

Ceilings are an often-overlooked blank canvas. It's not the norm to find intricately patterned ceilings in a bedroom in the United States, but in other parts of the globe, waking up to fabulous frescos, mosaics, or inlay is not uncommon. It makes great sense in a space designed for sleeping—given that the ceiling is the first and last view each day, why not take advantage of the surface area to create something beautiful to look at?

The several hotels featured here have incredibly intricate ceilings. At La Mamounia in Marrakech, historic ceilings were restored by hundreds of craftsmen and feature inlay, carvings, gilding, and tilework. For most of us, this isn't a design idea to re-create at home. But it would be easy to extract one motif and paint it in a room or to install a single perimeter line of tiles that hail from a particular place to bring back memories of travels—or to serve as inspiration for places you someday want to go. Another is to take cues from American designer, author, and hotelier Maryam Montague. At her hotel in Marrakech, she used a stencil based on Uzbek embroidery design to add pattern to a turquoise ceiling. Hanging a printed fabric from the ceiling as a canopy would be another way to wake up to a similar tapestry of color.

ABOVE: At Peacock Pavilions in Marrakech, owner and designer Maryam Montague commissioned a custom stencil based on a piece of Uzbek embroidery to adorn the ceiling. With the ready-made stencils and scanning techniques available today, it would be easy to create one at home.

OPPOSITE: The design of the Camel Bone Weave Moroccan Stencil was created by Royal Design Studio for designer Maryam Montague. The design greets guests when they wake up in the guest room of Montague's Moroccan hotel, Peacock Pavilions.

OVERLEAF, LEFT: It's impossible to imagine waking up to a more dazzling ceiling than this one at La Mamounia in Marrakech. Designer Jacques Garcia worked with thousands of craftsmen to restore the eighteenth-century former palace, re-creating mosaics, handcarved and painted ceilings, inlaid doors, crafted tile, and carved plaster. While it's not something to easily recreate at home, the star motifs could inspire a unique design.

OVERLEAF, RIGHT: One of the most amazing things about Moroccan architecture and design is that everything is embellished. All surfaces—floors, ceilings, columns, walls—are treated as an opportunity to create something beautiful. This room at La Sultana in Marrakech showcases Moroccan style at its most glorious, but any single pattern from here could serve as inspiration for design motifs to bring home.

Calm Retreats

One of the joys of checking into a hotel is taking a vacation not just from your own city, but from the clutter of everyday life. Bills, stacks of magazines, school projects, toys, papers, loose change, and other household culprits of mess are nowhere to be found. Instead, hotel rooms are oases of order and cleanliness—at least when you check in. What's key is the powerful effect that being in a space free of disorder can have. It simply makes you feel relaxed.

If you want to bring some of that Zen into your daily life, the first step is creating at least an illusion of a clutter-free space. Especially in a bedroom, it's important to get rid of all those small things that keep you up at night. Electronic devices and to-do lists should all be contained in another room. Furniture should be minimal—a cozy chair or sofa, side tables, and a bed are sometimes all that is needed. Invest in

closed storage, keep shelves and tabletops free of anything but the essentials that a hotel would have—music, books, flowers, water.

Another step toward achieving serenity in a bedroom is finding a color palette that makes you instantly feel calm. For some that's a rich, dark hue, but for others more muted tones—grays, beiges, creams—are the shades that relax. For bedding, hotels have a go-to color palette: white. While patterned sheets can be fun, white sheets offer a visual break in room that's soothing and easy. Plus there's no worrying about whether they go with anything else you introduce.

LEFT, ABOVE: This guest room at Le Royal Monceau-Raffles in Paris, designed by Philippe Starck, demonstrates that soothing spaces don't have to be boring. Rather than bathe the room completely in gray, he painted rectangles on the walls, "framed" by areas of white—an easy but fresh treatment. The bed is also placed in the middle of the room, making it feel almost like a stage. An Arne Jacobsen Egg Chair from 1958, covered in cognac leather, fills a corner, providing womb-like seating for taking in the view or for strumming the acoustic guitar placed in each room.

ABOVE: This dreamy bedroom at Canal House in Amsterdam features a Liberty print headboard that echoes the room's muted palette while providing a little pattern. Beige, cream, gray, and brown are featured throughout. Note also the small-space design trick of keeping the chest of drawers the same color as the walls—this makes the piece recede so the room feels larger.

OVERLEAF: At the Aman Tokyo, the floor, furniture, and closet doors are all in the same gorgeous wood tone, creating a visually unified space without the distraction of different colors and patterns. In addition, an all-in-one piece for the bed, side tables, and headboard adds to the unified, serene look.

All-white bedrooms and baths, like this one at Babylonstoren's Farm Hotel in South Africa, are the default option for relaxing spaces. To keep it interesting, however, the designers chose a clean-lined canopy bed with a simple, sheer, top panel and an oversized white steel tub from Lavo.

Gorgeous light-gray walls with simple boiserie highlight the forms of black bouillotte lamps, a brass chair, and rich wood floors. The combination of neutrals adds up to a sophisticated-yet-serene retreat at the Michele Bonan–designed Portrait Firenze in Italy.

Christiane Lemieux

FOUNDER OF DWELLSTUDIO

Favorite Hotel: Kashbah Tamadot, Marrakech, Morocco

I love experience. The best hotels in the world understand that full immersion is fundamental to real excellence. The best hotels go way beyond lodging. The Kasbah Tamadot is absolutely amazing because it hits all the senses. From the breathtaking setting in the Atlas Mountains to the perfectly appointed Berber tents, and topped off by Eve Branson's foundation that helps local artisans, the Kasbah checks absolutely every box. If I were going to open my perfect hotel, I would model it after this one.

Best Part of the Overall Design

All of the details are perfect. The recently renovated structure keeps the gorgeous intrinsic details and deeply beautiful Moroccan elements like a perfect tiled hammam, gorgeous reflecting pool, and the original carved doors—but it adds the modern amenities you would expect from Richard Branson. The design takes the best elements of local craftsmanship and beautifully blends everything into very sophisticated design. The hotel makes you feel like an explorer—in very high style. It's a fantasy, and that makes it truly memorable.

Best Space

The terraced outdoor spaces are absolutely spectacular. From the pool to the lounging areas with the vista of the Atlas Mountains—it is absolutely one of my most unforgettable hotel moments.

Best Parts of the Room

My room was a Berber tent fitted with all the elements of a luxury hotel room—from the lighting to a turndown service with Moroccan roses every night. Each tent also has a beautiful terrace overlooking the mountains.

Most Unexpected Design Element

The terraced lounge to the pool. It's dotted with pillows and outdoor tents. Absolutely stunning.

Design Inspiration You Brought Home

I absolutely love the doors in this hotel. It was a big revelation to me that a door could be an ornament, like a piece of jewelry, to a room that's otherwise beautifully spare and restrained. I love the contrast that creates. The design tension is amazing. I have absolutely internalized that.

DINING ROOMS
AND KITCHENS

Sculptural Spaces

One thing interior designers do well in kitchens and dining rooms is to think beyond what is simply practical. The focus is on what looks gorgeous, what would draw you in, what would make you want to enjoy being in those spaces. Comfort and practicality of course play into it, but the look is often the primary motivation. It's something to think about when designing a home space, even a practical one like a kitchen. Too often we talk ourselves out of a design decision that would be unexpected because we worry about making a mistake. This is how beige rooms happen. There is a bravery in hotel design that more of us would do well to emulate— we should feel empowered to make a statement in our own homes. The kitchens and dining rooms featured here provide an inspired range of ideas for how to decorate some of the busiest spaces in your life.

When you think about it, dining spaces really only have to feature three basic components: a table, chairs, and lighting. But they get such heavy use that adding elements of fun or whimsy will make every meal that much more memorable. To add character, designers often focus their creativity on walls and upholstery. Power prints on wallpaper, rich paint colors, and eye-catching chair fabrics are surefire ways to make a dining room distinctive. However, there's another option that's more subtle perhaps, but equally powerful: sculptural furniture. Think chairs with gorgeous curves in unexpected silhouettes, lighting that's more Calder than fluorescent, and tables with beautiful lines. Design-forward hotels like the India Mahdavi–designed Condesa DF in Mexico or the Brücke 49 in Switzerland don't miss an opportunity to champion original furniture and accessories. These hotels showcase museum-worthy pieces from maestros like Hans Wegner and Charles and Ray Eames in their dining spaces, demonstrating how to live with great design in real life.

PREVIOUS PAGES: At the San Giorgio on the Greek island of Mykonos, wood furniture pops against the crisp white walls that are so prevalent in Greek design. The rustic, casual hotel lobby offers accessible inspiration for a relaxed dining space. A vintage table is paired with a long bench on one side and assorted wood stools on the other. Basket pendant lights make a statement without overpowering the space.

ABOVE: Custom-designed plastic chairs at Casa Fayette in Mexico are contemporary takes on traditional Mexican *equipales* chairs. Their striking silhouettes and head-turning shade of green make them the signature element in this courtyard.

OPPOSITE: Designer India Mahdavi incorporated multiples—of Moooi's fiberglass Random Lights and her own Bishop bar stools— to make a statement based on rounded forms at the Condesa DF bar in Mexico City. The curves of the stools play off the circular lights beautifully. Painting both the ceiling and the walls turquoise ensures the white pendant lights stand out when viewed from every angle.

LEFT: Eames-style molded plastic chairs add a stylish and unexpectedly modern edge at an otherwise rustic restaurant at Casa Las Tortugas, a beachside hotel on Isla Holbox, just off the north tip of the Yucatán Peninsula in Mexico.

ABOVE: At Brücke 49, a bed-and-breakfast in the mountains of Switzerland, pared-down, modernist-style furniture meets Nordic flair with sheepskins from Muubs draped over Hans Wegner's CH33 chairs. For seamless style, the table from Copenhagen Joinery was created with legs that mirror the chairs.

Cozy and Captivating

One of the great joys of vacation is lingering over an amazing meal and a bottle of wine, talking away the night. It's a contrast to daily life, where meals are more often rushed. But what if you designed your dining space to be a space you didn't want to leave quickly? What if, instead of uncomfortable plastic chairs, you invested in generously proportioned armchairs that envelop you in velvet, as they do at No. 131 in the Cotswolds? What about adding a banquette in the teeny corner of your kitchen inspired by the Marquis Faubourg Saint-Honoré in Paris? Would maximizing the space in a refreshing way make you use it more? Adding a plush cushion and soft pillows, like designer Michele Bonan did, might just be the thing to make you actually sit down and eat breakfast. It could also become a spot where your kids want to do homework while you prep dinner, or a place for friends to gather after work. It could become so much more than just another kitchen table.

Hotel restaurant designers spend a lot of time thinking about how to get guests to stay a little longer, order a little more, and return. Creating beckoning spaces with rich, touchable textures, lovely colors, and pillows is one way they entice clients. So why not incorporate some of those ideas into your home life? You'll find that everyone may want to relax and linger over a great meal at your dining table, too.

OPPOSITE: At Ett Hem in Stockholm, a library is combined with a dining room. A generously proportioned red wing chair offers a place to curl up with a book, while vintage Kaare Klint leather chairs that add a clubby feel surround the dining table. A Lindsey Adelman chandelier casts a soft glow over the space and keeps the look current.

ABOVE: Shelves full of great art books, an elegant fireplace, and velvet banquettes and pillows at the Marquis Faubourg Saint-Honoré add up to one of the chicest and coziest spots to eat in Paris. The look could be replicable in any living room with an underused nook next to a mantel.

Director-style chairs in a sandy hue and a rope chandelier conjure up the nautical spirit of Kennebunkport, Maine, at The Tides Beach Club. Paired with a small circular table, the easy arrangement would work well in any nook to create a chic, beachy feeling.

LEFT: Leather chairs in an interesting, unexpected olive green and a table with nail-head trim provide a reassuringly traditional note in a dining room at the Lucky Onion No. 131 in the Cotswolds; the chandelier adds a bit of shimmer for glamour and creates aesthetic tension with the antique mirror on the far wall.

LEFT, BELOW: Turquoise walls, blue velvet seat cushions, orange leather chairs, and yellow curtains— the restaurant at J.K. Place Roma is an enchanting mix of saturated gem tones. The plush banquette is the perfect seating option for those who love long dinners.

OPPOSITE, TOP: Save space and make a dining area more interesting by taking a cue from the Chalet Pelerin in the French Alps and replacing half a dining room's chairs with a corner bench. No. 12 Interiors designers Blake Pike and Jane Hines had the banquette custom built to fit the antique French Savoyard table so the bench height would work perfectly.

OPPOSITE, BOTTOM: Take advantage of a dining room with an interesting view by creating a built-in seating area piled high with pillows, like this supremely comfortable nook at the Malliouhana in Anguilla.

Understated Spaces

Not all spaces need to scream for attention. Rooms that feature quiet palettes, classic shapes, and minimal embellishment are just as key to creating a mood as bolder ones. These spots create an immediate sense of calm, offering a respite from the outside world or a break from other rooms with more attention-seeking design.

Many designers seem to understand implicitly that when a hotel is located in a place with breathtaking scenery, the interiors don't need to compete with the beauty outside the window. If you have an enviable backdrop, why not take an understated approach to design?

A white or pale gray backdrop won't compete with a vibrant cityscape or the vivid colors in a tropical location, like Brazil's. When everything is blossoming outside, there is joy in a simple wood farmhouse table, easy flea market chairs, and classic silhouettes that are all well suited for rustic-chic dining rooms.

OPPOSITE: In a bright, white space a rich wood table and chairs provide a stunning contrast and a splash of green. A few palm fronds give a tropical sensibility, as in this former fishing cottage that has been transformed into the Uxua Casa Hotel & Spa in Brazil.

ABOVE: A collection of ceramic pendant lights with different forms by local artisans in Brazil adds the requisite amount of personality to this simple dining space at the Uxua Casa Hotel.

LEFT, ABOVE: Just three colors—white, black, and green—give a simple dining room plenty of pattern and moxie at the Lombardi House in Hollywood.

LEFT, BELOW: Eating on cushions at low-lying tables is common practice in many countries, including India, where the Raas DeviGarh is located. Why not recreate the chairless dining concept for your own gathering space? It's more relaxed, less expensive, and offers a more global take on the dining room.

OPPOSITE, TOP: Single-wall kitchens are a fact of city life, but they can be an eyesore in a small, open space unless they feel somewhat designed. At Palihouse West Hollywood, the navy backsplash, open shelves, marble counters, and black cabinets look sophisticated.

OPPOSITE, BELOW: The clean, geometric lines of midcentury furniture are on full display at The Hoxton, in Amsterdam. With the white backdrop and pared-down design, the rich, warm wood details and forms hold their own.

OVERLEAF: Sometimes playing off a design drawback can turn it into a strength. At The Boro Hotel in Long Island City, for example, architects Grzywinski+Pons emphasized the prevalence of concrete instead of trying to conceal its grittiness. The look is modern and monochromatic, with everything from the table to the lighting in gray tones but unexpected shapes.

DINING ROOMS AND KITCHENS

Fearless Color

If you are looking for a showstopping design, hotels are the best source. Unlike that voice of worry that creeps in when you are designing your own home, wondering if a choice will be too much for everyday living, hotel designers have the freedom of designing a space that's supposed to impress and intrigue at first sight. Nothing is too much when the goal is to stand out.

For example, at the Suján Rajmahal in Jaipur, walls are covered in a print that can only be described as an ode to pink. Not content with stopping there, they painted the ceiling in the hue as well. Even better, they brought in beautiful white chairs with an intriguing cutout design that underscores the repeat of the pattern on the walls. Could a smaller version of that space look as amazing in Indiana as it does in India?

For sure. The room is a reminder not to hold back next time you want to make a bold move. Big, crazy design ideas are sometimes too fun to talk yourself out of—and they'll always be memorable and meaningful.

OPPOSITE: For a dramatic, modern dining space try a dark, graphic wallpaper like this one from Arte that features slightly different shades of textured blue in abstract forms. At the Hotel Henriette in Paris, a gorgeous vintage brass sconce punctuates the wall, doubling as both light and art.

ABOVE: There's no rule that says dining chairs have to match. At the recently revamped Hotel Bachaumont in Paris, designer Dorothée Meilichzon used four different patterns plus navy to upholster banquettes and chairs.

OPPOSITE: Whether they are anchoring opposite ends of a long rectangular table or just providing roomy seating for breakfast for two, wing chairs are an incredibly comfortable but unexpected option for a dining space. These versions at the J.K. Place Capri show that an abstract print, like this lavender ikat, makes their classic silhouette look fresh.

ABOVE: At Main on Nantucket, wide horizontal bands of navy stripes dominate the space and offer a playful take on nautical style. Seaweed prints and floral curtain fabric add a softer, balancing counterpoint.

OPPOSITE: At The Colony Palms Hotel, pattern rules. In the restaurant, Schumacher's Topkapi paper is behind the maroon banquette while Schumacher's Sultan's Trellis covers the wall to the left. Both prints feature motifs that are similar in style, and as they are in the same pomegranate colorway, they work together.

RIGHT: This dining room at the Suján Rajmahal in Jaipur, India, is a celebration of pink. Proving that you can't have too much of a good thing, an abstract wallpaper in shades of rose is paired with a glossy, hot-pink ceiling. Sculptural white cutout chairs and white marble floors balance out the intense hue.

A Nod to Classic Style

A few vintage and antique pieces can provide a sense of history and timelessness that a property with only new furniture never can. Whether they're blue-blooded antiques or a pair of chairs of less prestigious parentage scored at a flea market, there is a history that comes with older pieces that imbues a room with unmatchable character.

For spaces in historic properties, the challenge is how to make antiques feel fresh and how to incorporate them with newer additions. Those with pieces handed down from past generations should look to the storied Connaught in London, where faded chinoiserie cabinets were restored to their former glory, with a little twist—the upper halves of the cabinets were lined with mirrors and set up as chic dry bars that hold liquor, glasses, and snacks. It's truly a piece that honors the old while bringing in something new—definitely the best approach when designing with treasured heirloom pieces.

OPPOSITE, TOP: Vintage prints, like these of birds, look fresh when hung in a graphic display of multiples that share identical, simple frames. For the dining room at Canal House in Amsterdam, No. 12 Interiors customized a live edge oak table with a metal base, then paired it with simple black chairs.

OPPOSITE, BOTTOM: This antique chinoiserie cabinet has a secret. Designer Guy Oliver restored and repurposed the piece during the 2008 renovation of the Connaught in London, creating a charming mirrored dry bar inside the top half.

RIGHT: Play up the curves of a round antique table by repeating them elsewhere in a dining room. A tiered brass chandelier and chairs with curved backs echo a circular wood-and-marble table at Casas del XVI in the Dominican Republic, while framed architectural prints, a cabinet with classical detailing, and a collection of blue-and-white pottery reinforce the historic mood.

OVERLEAF: This chic dining space at No. 131 in the Cotswolds counterintuitively pairs tufted wing chairs with a small, simple table. Upholstered in soft velvet, the curved chairs invite diners to curl up and enjoy a long, leisurely dinner.

Small and Chic Kitchens

Kitchens are a lovely bonus in a hotel room. They instantly make a space feel more homey, even if all that means is having access to a fridge, a sink, some counter space, and real dishes. While most hotels don't include ovens, just having the ability to whip up a familiar snack during a long trip instead of calling room service is a simple luxury.

Since the square footage allotted to hotel kitchen areas is usually not much, however, designers have come up with some pretty clever ideas for those living in small spaces. Studio apartment dwellers should take note of the Palihouse and Hotel Bachaumont versions, which occupy a single wall in an aesthetically interesting way. These smart alternatives to a galley kitchen allow space to be reallocated to living and dining areas.

A kitchen or bar area needs to reflect the style of the surrounding room when it's visible from adjacent spaces— the transition between kitchen and living areas needs to be seamless. For example, Ace Hotel Downtown Los Angeles has masculine and polished finishes while the kitchen at Bert's Box features wood cabinets with the same rustic feel as the vintage wood planks that line the walls.

Good ideas for enlivening a small kitchen can also be found throughout hotels' dining and entertaining areas. Hotel bars, restaurants, and cafés, especially those with tile work and backsplashes, can be full of ideas that can be applied at home. The vibrant hand-painted tiles in two tones at the American Trade Hotel in Panama would look pretty for delineating space in any kitchen, for example. Similarly, the cement subway tiles and copper bar stools at The Boro Hotel café in Long Island City would be amazing in any city kitchen—especially a loft.

While the kitchen island has become ubiquitous in modern kitchen design, Ilse Crawford paired this vintage wood table and chairs with a built-in bench for a homier and dual-purpose alternative at Ett Hem in Stockholm.

RIGHT: Colorful, elaborate tile is a trend that's making a comeback. The pretty floors at the American Trade Hotel bar in Panama show how simply using different colorways of the same pattern rev up any space.

OPPOSITE: Combine graphic, industrial, and inexpensive treatments like these cement subway tiles with a couple of statement bar stools for a look that's decidedly downtown. Placed vertically along a backsplash or on an island, like here at the café at the Boro Hotel in Long Island City, the tiles look clean and contemporary. Copper Real Good bar chairs by Blu Dot provide a sculptural perch and a textural contrast.

OPPOSITE, BELOW: To make a small kitchen feel like more of a retreat than a crammed-in functional space, keep the palette light and monochromatic—on floors, cabinets, and even plates—as they did at the Scarp Ridge Lodge in Crested Butte, Colorado.

LEFT: Colorful tile is an easy and inexpensive way to jazz up your standard white kitchen. At La Minervetta Maison in Sorrento, Italy, aqua-blue tile paired with red-and-white striped chairs instantly creates nautical zing, made even more fun with colorful and mismatched table settings.

OPPOSITE, ABOVE: Brick herringbone floors and unfinished wood cabinets are updated with an alluring gray-green wall and openwork shelving at this kitchen in the French Alps, at Chalet Pelerin—a great option for any rural second home or cabin.

OPPOSITE, BELOW: Expertly curated open shelves at The Hoxton in Amsterdam showcase sculptural pottery and vintage glassware against a backdrop of reclaimed wood. This design idea would be well suited to a second-home kitchen—or to highly organized owners.

RIGHT: In kitchen design, where the formula is pretty standard, any unexpected textures, finishes, or details make a space unique. The striking contrast of polished brass fixtures, dark wood cabinets, and marble counters at the Ace Hotel Downtown Los Angeles endow even a small sliver of kitchen with a hip, masculine vibe.

RIGHT, BELOW: Bert's Box at The Pig Hotel features cabinets in a similar dark, rustic wood as the walls, which helps the kitchen recede. The living room is delineated by a small sisal rug, paisley armchairs, and a green velvet ottoman facing out toward the floor-to-ceiling windows. Chevron tiles on floors and in a strip on walls keep the mood light.

OPPOSITE, TOP: A grid tile floor, a bold and unexpected color choice for the cabinets, a couple of interesting lights, and fun bar stools can give the smallest of kitchens plenty of punch, like this space at The Hoxton in Amsterdam.

OPPOSITE, BELOW: Marble built-in shelves make guests take notice of this chic wet bar at the Hotel Bachaumont in Paris, and the look would translate well to any studio apartment kitchen. In an open floor plan, making kitchen colors and materials match the style of the rest of the pad is a smart move.

Joe Lucas
DESIGNER AND OWNER OF HARBINGER LA

Favorite Hotel: The Battery, San Francisco, California

I love staying here. It's a private social club that also has rooms. A good designer friend of mine is a member, so I stay as his guest. It was designed by Ken Fulk and is gorgeous. I love the club feel of it all and it's by far the chicest place to stay in the city.

Best Parts of the Overall Design

I feel very at home when I am there, thanks to the mood. The dining and bar areas are comfortable and cool. Lots of low seating areas, great big booths to eat in, and a beautiful bar that grounds the center of the space. The incredibly high ceilings and industrial vibe mix well with the wood finishes and steel doors and windows. Great music is always pumping in, and Ken has added in unique design elements with some old maritime art and fabulous light fixtures.

Best Space

There is a beautiful little courtyard at the back of the club that lends itself well to just hanging out for a cocktail or grabbing a morning coffee and breakfast on the patio. In a big, bustling city, it is always nice to have a quiet haven outdoors without the noise.

Most Unexpected Elements:

The food is fantastic. The bar and restaurants are right in the middle when you enter, so they become a very important factor in the overall vibe. Then they also have a beautiful fitness center, spa, and locker rooms, and the design elements there are just as special as in the rest of the space. Ken didn't let any part go without specific attention to the design.

Best Parts of the Rooms

The bedrooms almost have a French 1940s feel to them thanks to the mix of leather and cerused oak details. They have a very masculine-but-classic mood; mixed velvets, wools, and great wood finishes bring it all together.

Design Inspiration Brought Home

I love the industrial and sleek design of the building's steel stair rails and windows. I think it adds so much interior architecture to a space to have something simple but visual in the common areas.

LIVING SPACES

Dark Means Dramatic

When hotelier Sean MacPherson opened The Ludlow on the Lower East Side of Manhattan, he said that he wanted the hotel to serve as a living room for the neighborhood. Walk in at any point today, and you can see that he succeeded. Groups of people are having work meetings on the curvy, 1970s-style couches, visiting couples are planning their city adventures under gilded lighting, and creative types are writing masterpieces on their laptops, coffee—or cocktail—in hand. The music is thumping, the seating is comfortable, the libations are amazing, so of course you would want it to be your living room. And that's the brilliance of the gesture right there: the best hotel design feels like some place you would want to really live in.

Many boutique hotels design their lobbies to feel like living rooms with the same personal details you would find in a home—unique art, vintage furniture, books, accessories, and comfortable pieces you want to lounge in. It reinforces the idea that you aren't staying in a hotel, but a home.

The lobby at The Jerome in Aspen is a case in point. Interior designer Todd-Avery Lenahan revamped the c. 1889 hotel, honoring its history and collection of art and antiques while bringing the spaces up to date with new fabrics and paint. Caramel leather Chesterfield sofas anchor the room next to an oversized portrait of the hotel's founder, Jerome B. Wheeler, and a roaring fireplace. A rich, deep gray shade envelopes the space, making it feel cozy, warm, and very personal.

Dark walls are a powerful design tool, especially if you have a lot of vintage pieces. Against deeper walls, colors and patterns become more vibrant, art pops, and details you don't want noticed, like worn furniture, are overshadowed by the strong color. It should be your go-to if you want to make an impact in a space without spending a lot of money.

PREVIOUS PAGES: Designer Ilse Crawford chose a moody gray-green for the living spaces at the house-hotel Ett Hem in Stockholm. By keeping the couch and curtains in similar shades and rest of the space in dark tones, the color's effect is enhanced.

RIGHT: It's not an easy job revamping a storied nineteenth-century hotel valued for its antiques and history. Designer Todd-Avery Lenahan honored the legacy of Aspen's Hotel Jerome by keeping its traditional pieces. He updated the space by injecting dynamic, modern finds such as a Lucite coffee table and a graphic rug composed of stripes of different widths, shades, and textures of navy. Sidewalk-gray walls are dark enough to cast a spotlight on the quirky collection of furniture, but light enough to keep the space feeling airy.

LEFT: Designer Kit Kemp uses another option for achieving dark walls: upholstering them with fabric. The effect is softer, warmer, and more alluring than paint. At this suite at the Crosby Street Hotel, a gorgeous deep aubergine fabric is paired with crisp, white trim.

ABOVE AND BELOW: Every design detail is the same in these suites designed by Michele Bonan at the Marquis Faubourg Saint-Honoré in Paris—except for the paint color. The same space looks classically elegant in beige, but moody and modern in charcoal.

The Genius of Stripes

In the late 1990s, the hotel lobby was reimagined. Following the success of boutique hotels like Miami's Delano and Manhattan's Morgans Hotel that paired nightlife with hotel living, Starwood launched the W Hotel in Manhattan. It was the first major chain to recast the lobby as a social hub. Guests emerged from elevators to find dim lights, blasting dance music, and cocktails flowing. Try and enter today's like-minded institutions from the outside, and you might find a velvet rope and a line. With cool furniture, conversation-starting art, DJs, and a glamorous crowd, hotel lobbies became bars/nightclubs/gathering spaces. Design and art were key players in that transformation. It was a genius idea: why not keep hotel guests in house, and make it appealing enough to lure the locals too?

But what can popular hotel lobbies teach you about home design? So much. For starters, they are notoriously high-traffic spaces. Their designers use prints, stripes, and dark palettes in both upholstery and carpets to conceal wear, tear, and spills. Think of stripes in particular as a savvy solution to a variety of design problems. Furniture a little blah? Upholster it in a bold stripe to make it an instant statement piece. Boring space? Stripes instantly add a dose of fun. Room too narrow? Throw a striped rug on the floor with the lines arranged horizontally where you want the space to feel wider. House's main thoroughfare? Stripes on the floor can help hide dirt.

Stripes are the chameleons of design, so it's not a surprise that they show up in a range of hotel spaces with different design styles. They can project any mood depending on their color, width, and quantity. Wide stripes easily become a focal point, so color choice is key. For example, at Malliouhana in Anguilla, bright yellow-and-white-striped pillows inject a carefree, happy energy. At Grace Bay Club on Turks and Caicos, an oversized rug's pattern captures the Caribbean spirit too, but the choice of gray keeps the look sophisticated. At the house-hotel Ett Hem in Stockholm, black-and-white vertical stripes paired with dramatic charcoal-green walls and modernist furniture add up to a living room of understated cool. There is truly a stripe for every occasion.

At the house-hotel Ett Hem in Stockholm, a boxy sofa upholstered in wide black-and-white stripes provides the perfect complement to the curves of a vintage chair by Italian designer Tobia Scarpa.

TOP: Oversize, striped carpets can be found everywhere from Ikea to high-end showrooms, which speaks to their powerful effect on space. In this room at the Grace Bay Club in Turks and Caicos, they draw the eye straight out to the view.

ABOVE: While this open-air living room is at the Lamai Serengeti in Tanzania, the playful design relying on symmetry and stripes could be be re-created in a city apartment or a small living room anywhere.

Designer Michele Bonan has made the J.K. Place Capri one of the most glamorous hotels in Italy. The cliffside spot features the sharp, quintessentially Mediterranean contrast colors of navy and white. The rug of assorted stripes visually widens the space and injects subtle pattern and just enough color.

109

Elegant Exotic

One of the hallmarks of a beautifully designed hotel is that it is reflective of its location without resorting to cliché. Of course you want your hotel in Marrakech to capture that country's colorful, exotic passion, but you don't want to feel like you are in some sort of Moroccan theme park. The most alluring hotels maintain a careful balance between sophisticated, creative design and local inspiration. It's one of the reasons why the idea of bringing a little bit of Paris back to Poughkeepsie or conjuring up India in Illinois isn't so farfetched. To remind yourself of a visit to an exotic location, you don't need to re-create your hotel room exactly at home, just to inject one or two notes of inspiration unique to that location into the design. The blend means you'll be creating something all your own—a space that doesn't exist anywhere else in the world.

The carefree, stylish vibe of the beachfront city of Miami is captured in the design of this living space at 1 Hotel South Beach. Meyer Davis Studio designed a room that will help guests unwind in style. Low-profile sofas and ottomans encourage putting your feet up. A white backdrop punctuated by sea-inspired art echoes the beautiful view outside, while soothing tones evoke a Zen tranquility.

OPPOSITE, TOP: This open-air living space at Amandari in Bali features a Balinese-style roof and an updated take on the built-in sofas and bolsters that are hallmarks of Indonesian design. Incorporating rattan or teak furniture with a copious amount of pillows could bring a subtle hint of Southeast Asia home.

OPPOSITE, BELOW: The spirit of all the Aman resorts is one of total Zen. At the Amanoi in Vietnam, that calm effect is achieved by keeping the design spare, the palette muted, and the furnishings symmetrical.

RIGHT: At Peacock Pavilions in Marrakech, designer and owner Maryam Montague created an eclectic mix that projects a global vibe. A vintage Indian mirror and Frank Gehry Wiggle Chairs bring sculptural flair to the space. The couch is upholstered in a vintage Moroccan wool blanket with bolsters that pair Belgian velvet and African textiles.

LEFT: This archway, which frames a cozy seating nook at the Jnane Tamsna in Marrakech, could add some exotic flair if re-created in a home den.

ABOVE: French designer Jacques Garcia paired a mix of Moroccan elements—an arched doorway, painted doors, and tiled floors—with European touches like Venetian mirrors, floral prints, and Louis XV chairs at La Mamounia in Marrakech. Every surface, whether it is the floor or the walls, features exquisite design flourishes. Cream fabric draped on walls, the red velvet headboard, and the plaster carvings combine to create an effect that is simply magical.

One Bold Move

Hotels are the best source of fearless decorating ideas because they often use design to differentiate themselves from the competition. When translating major design moves from hotel to home, remember not to re-create the look exactly, but to scale it to everyday reality: what works in a space with high ceilings and lots of square footage may not work in the burbs. The trick is to focus on re-creating just one impressive exclamation point from a hotel, not ten.

This group of hotel spaces showcases the power of making one bold move. Sometimes all it takes is one confident choice to make a memorable or emotional impact. In a living room, that could be going with an unexpected piece of art, a powerful color, a showstopping print on upholstery, or standout furniture.

Casas del XVI in the Dominican Republic, decorated by Patricia Reid, is a great example of how to make a commercial-scale design statement work in real life. The conversation-starting poppy-red hue of the walls avoids being overwhelming because it's paired with shades of brown. The instinctual move would be to inject a neutral by keeping the furniture white, but that would actually contrast too much with red. Furniture in neutral and brown shades and in linen and leather balances out the color while keeping the look sophisticated and exotic. An embroidered fabric panel hung as art features the same shade of red in its pattern—by having the art echo the bold color, rather than introducing yet another hue, the art works with the vibrant red, not against it.

OPPOSITE: A deep gray-blue makes a large lounge area feel cocooning and intimate for guests coming in from the Manhattan streets at the Baccarat Hotel and Residences. Paris-based design duo Gilles & Boissier incorporated custom Baccarat crystal chandeliers with pleated shades to punctuate the dark envelope with some dazzle.

ABOVE: In a room otherwise filled with earth tones at the Hotel Jerome in Aspen, adding a vibrant red rug might seem counterintuitive. However, not only is the design of the Navajo-inspired rug eye-catching and thematic for the Western location, the pattern adds color and is a good choice for a high-traffic area.

OPPOSITE, TOP: One bright green chair injects all the levity and energy in a living area at the Field Guide in Stowe, Vermont—just imagine how different the room would look with the same chair in brown. A vibrant color and a vintage shape might be all a space needs to feel fresh.

OPPOSITE, BELOW: Pattern is the easiest way to revive older furniture, as this yellow-and-white print demonstrates at the Freehand Hotel in Miami.

THIS PAGE, TOP: Wood-paneled living spaces were a hallmark of 1970s design. At Edson Hill in Vermont, design firm Gauthier Stacy lightened and glammed up the space with a black-and-white Moroccan shag carpet, a custom cream bench, a white-framed mirror, and gold-leaf wood coffee tables.

THIS PAGE, BELOW: Casas del XVI in the Dominican Republic proves that a red living room is possible. The trick to making the color appealing and not overpowering is to pair it with neutral-but-dark furniture. Another smart choice is selecting art that features the same red shade—it works with instead of against the strong color.

Striking a Playful Note

Today, we use living rooms for everything from eating to entertaining to lounging to working and for doing homework. Perhaps because they are often such multipurpose spaces, there is an almost innate inclination to keep living rooms neutral while allowing smaller rooms—dining rooms, bathrooms, and children's rooms—to have all the fun. Why not make your own living space more playful? There are already plenty of "greige" living rooms in the world.

Take a cue from Manhattan's Crosby Street Hotel and cover your walls in a large-scale, printed fabric paired with two of the world's happiest hues for upholstery—orange and lime green. If you already have an otherwise-subdued space in place, perhaps one including a gray couch and white walls, the Palihouse Santa Monica shows how you can shake it up by adding a hilarious print and a burst of hot pink. As several of these spaces show, adding one or two side chairs covered in a bright, cheerful fabric can go a long way toward perking up a room. Color and pattern are the keys here. Unlock and have fun.

Mod furniture and a fun beehive print in a cheery shade of aqua liven up a living space at the Oceana Beach Club Hotel in Santa Monica, California.

THIS PAGE, TOP: Rev up a space with a workhorse gray or beige couch by pairing it with an armchair and ottoman upholstered in an unexpected pattern or color. At the Palihouse in Santa Monica a pink, quilted pouf and a peach-print side chair inject some levity.

THIS PAGE, BELOW: Designer Todd-Avery Lenahan's renovation of Malliouhana is a mix of throwback Hollywood Regency style and Anguilla's sunny mood. These vintage-inspired chairs show how to mix several textiles on one chair. Turquoise chairs feature beige linen seats and cushion, a colorful print on the back, and yellow-and-white striped throw pillows. The key when mixing prints is to pull out one color that links both, in this case a bright yellow.

OPPOSITE, TOP: Designer Kit Kemp is known for creating energy by mixing prints. At the Ham Yard Hotel in London, the trick is in pairing patterns that each feature one or more of four colors: navy, pink, gray, and light blue.

OPPOSITE, BELOW: Designer Martyn Lawrence Bullard's showstopping interiors for the Casa Laguna Hotel & Spa in Laguna Beach were inspired by the beach and the Spanish Colonial architecture of the early-twentieth-century property. Moorish tiles and ceramics in large-scale patterns line the walls and the star motif in the tiles is repeated in the Morovian star lighting. Periwinkle banquettes create beckoning corner seating nooks, and the choice of blue throughout is a nod to the beachside community and the colors of sea and sky.

Art That Makes a Statement

Selecting art is often one of the last choices people make when decorating a room, but it's one of the most important—some would say the single most important. Art sets the tone for a space more effectively than any style of furniture ever will. It can make a traditionally decorated room feel more modern, or introduce either some gravitas or levity, depending on the piece.

Pinterest boards would have you believe that gallery walls are the go-to choice for residential spaces. Hotels, on the other hand, often select oversize statement pieces for public spaces. It makes sense: they have large walls to fill and one outsize piece will stand out better than many tiny ones to set mood. The takeaway here is to observe how one big painting can actually make a space look larger—residential or commercial. As the art expands, so does the eye. Don't be intimidated by something larger than a poster-size piece, even in a smallish room.

The lobby design at The Brice in Savannah, Georgia, is crisp and edited, an intriguing combination of glamour, comfort, and fun. A black-and-white painting by artist Lydia Hwang in that same spirit is a piece that rules the room.

THIS PAGE, TOP:
A wood-paneled living room is brightened up with light furniture and a colorful abstract painting by artist Sarah Hinckley at the Hotel Edson in Vermont— a great tip for anyone looking to update a cabin.

THIS PAGE, BELOW:
Art can be culled from nature, as this stunning example at the eco-friendly 1 Hotel Central Park proves. Artist Shinichi "Miya" Miyazaki's oversized maple tree root becomes the focal point of a seating area.

OPPOSITE, ABOVE:
Symmetry reigns in the lobby of the J.K. Place Roma. A showstopping, oversize abstract painting emphasizes the tones and lines found elsewhere in the room.

OPPOSITE, BELOW: At the glamorous Portrait Firenze hotel, designer Michele Bonan placed an oversized mirror behind a sofa, then hung a framed black-and-white photograph directly on top of it. The mirror makes the space feel larger and helps to reflect more light into the space.

John Robshaw

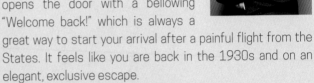

Favorite Hotel: The Imperial Hotel, New Delhi, India

At the entrance a tall, turbaned Sikh opens the door with a bellowing "Welcome back!" which is always a great way to start your arrival after a painful flight from the States. It feels like you are back in the 1930s and on an elegant, exclusive escape.

Best Parts of the Overall Design

Marble, marble, marble all over the place! Marble lines the long hallways, the rooms, the restaurants. I can't get enough of it. The lighting comes from old colonial ceiling lights set dim enough to relax you. Old Rajasthani miniature paintings and historic prints on the walls create a fun gallery as you walk to your room.

Best Space

I love the massive swimming pool. There's an obelisk right there in the middle, with a fountain pouring out as birds drink. It's surrounded by red sandstone walkways and huge palms sway above. I find myself there most afternoons, having a chai and hiding from the city.

Best Parts of the Room

The room I like has a massive bed to unwind in and a huge wooden bureau for all of your clothes. There's also a lovely old writing desk that looks out onto the gardens. It is always the same, and I am always happy to be back.

Most Unexpected Design Element

The Imperial is a part of India's past, and they've done a great job of preserving that without encapsulating it. The rooms have been updated with modern needs but still have old colonial beds, chairs, and dressers. You could never try to re-create the history of a hotel like this and get it right. It's a blast to stay in.

Design Inspiration Brought Home

The Spice Route restaurant is full of massive teak columns—to the point where you have to pay attention to where you're stepping as you walk through—but I think it creates a magical space for dining.

BATHROOMS

The Bath in the Bedroom

One of the great luxuries of a hotel stay is often the bathroom. Guests get to experience amazing features that aren't in the average home: deep soaking tubs with grand views, outdoor showers, ceiling murals, mosaic tile, or stunning slabs of marble or stone. Like anyone with a small space, however, hotels have to be clever about how to maximize every available inch. To make rooms feel less cramped, many hotels are minimizing—or forgoing—the bathroom walls and incorporating a bath or shower into the overall main bedroom design, which can make a space feel larger. With so many gorgeous tubs and creative shower ideas available, having the bath be part of your bedroom can really add to the space's appeal. There is something so lovely about the idea of lounging in a hot bath, then putting on a robe and crawling directly into bed. Why not re-create the luxury at home? It truly gives the sensation that your bedroom is your own private escape, not just a place for sleeping at the end of long work days.

Be forewarned—this takes some thoughtful preparation to be carried off well. For starters, you need to decide if you want a bathtub or shower. The shower option automatically feels a little more contemporary. At 1 Hotel Central Park, the first thing you'll notice when you walk in the room is a stunning glass-and-metal enclosed shower. The boxy space is set around one marble wall—a contemporary way to include the classic bath material. At The Hoxton in Holborn, London, they've made the shower the focal point by using cherry-red subway tiles. Set next to a vampy, partially nude portrait, a raw wood desk, and a metal Emeco chair, the look feels very James Bond.

If you prefer a tub, choose a style that relates to your overall room design. At the romantic Borgo Santo Pietro in Tuscany, rooms feature antique chandeliers, nineteenth-century furniture, billowing silk curtains, and oversize hand-carved beds. In one guest room, tucked in a corner beside a landscape mural, is a porcelain claw-foot tub with a burnished metal exterior. A small side table holds toiletries and a mirrored sconce above provides light—the beautiful bathtub looks as at home as the rest of the antiques in the space. Vintage, sculptural, or metal tubs are all good choices for a bedroom. The key is that the bathtub should either have a beautiful shape, be made from an alluring material, or show an eye-catching color.

PAGES 130–31: Every detail of this Carrara-clad bathroom at The Greenwich Hotel is elegant: the rectangular marble slabs that beautifully envelop the room, the oversize soaking tub that you want to dive into, and the gray-and-white mosaic tile floor from Urban Archeology.

PREVIOUS PAGES: At 1 Hotel Central Park, instead of making the bathroom a separate, closed-off space the designers opted for an open glass, metal, and marble shower stall that gives the illusion of a larger room. For privacy, a curtain can be drawn between the two areas.

LEFT: Colorblocked pastel walls help frame a classic tub in a contemporary way in a guest room at The Chequit, on Shelter Island.

OPPOSITE, TOP: A claw-foot tub painted in a surprisingly bold red adds some unexpected zing to a guest room at No. 38, The Park, in the Cotswolds.

OPPOSITE, BELOW: A burnished metal claw-foot soaking tub fits right in with the taffeta curtains, antique furniture and sconces, and romantic landscape mural at the Borgo Santo Pietro in Tuscany.

Making a Bathtub the Focal Point

An exciting trend to emerge in the past few years is bathtubs so stunning that they rightfully stake a claim as the highlight of any space. New to the market are modern, sculptural versions that complement contemporary spaces as well as retro-inspired silhouettes that work with classic rooms. The range of materials and finishes is also staggering: stone, wood, marble, copper, bright paint. These tubs are so visually interesting that they often lead a room's design.

One of the most remarkable bathrooms ever is at the Estancia Vik, in Uruguay. Local jacaranda trees were used to craft the gorgeous, arched bath. But it doesn't stop there—the surrounding walls are crafted from the same warm wood so the space feels earthy and glamorous at once. Another stunning departure from the basic white bath is at Monteverdi, in Tuscany. Their oversize, black stone version is big enough for two and melds beautifully with the rustic wood floors and beams of a renovated eighteenth-century building. The combination of natural materials and the unexpected black stone makes it a star.

A striking example of how a tub can focus a view comes from the Auberge du Soleil in Napa Valley. When you walk into a light-filled room there, you look straight through it and out onto a lovely terrace and garden where a freestanding outdoor bath awaits under a slatted wood canopy that allows sunlight to hit the tub while providing privacy. The combination of the unexpected setting and the beautiful silhouette raises the bar for hotel baths everywhere. If you are lucky enough to live in a warm climate and your yard has some privacy, consider this original and luxurious idea.

To take advantage of a view from inside, emulate another emerging trend in hotel design that translates beautifully to home design: placing a tub right in the center of a window. At The Langham in Chicago, St. Regis in Abu Dhabi, Viña Vik in Chile, and the Southern Ocean Lodge in Australia, you'll find bathtubs placed underneath or next to an expansive window. It's a gorgeous way to lay out a bathroom, and feels very current. For privacy without curtains, place the tub a few inches below the sill, as they did at the Field Guide in Vermont. At the high-rise St. Regis in Abu Dhabi, the tub is so large that it completely envelops the body, providing privacy in a decadent way. A splurge for sure, but an option if you want to keep the windows unobscured.

PREVIOUS PAGES, LEFT: Designer Marisabel Gómez Vázquez incorporated the same cement floor tiles in the bedrooms, terrace, and bathroom at The Cape in Los Cabos. The deep soaking tub for two here is the standout, placed in the center of the room for a more open feeling.

PREVIOUS PAGES, RIGHT: At Estancia Vik in Uruguay, designed by owners Carrie and Alex Vik, both the walls and the bathtub were sculpted from local jacaranda trees. The bath is curved and with one end higher to support the back comfortably.

OPPOSITE, TOP: The massive marble soaking tub designed by Studio Ilse for Ett Hem in Stockholm looks as much like a sculpture as a bathtub.

OPPOSITE, BOTTOM: When a bathroom is open to the bedroom, choosing warmer or more interesting options than ceramic tile helps the space feel like a glamorous extension of the rest of the space. Metallic wall tiles and a silver tub dazzle at No. 38, The Park in the Cotswolds.

ABOVE: Roman & Williams revamped the nineteenth-century Pearl Brewery to create the Hotel Emma in San Antonio, Texas. The combination of clawfoot tubs, brass fixtures, fig trees, and blue and white tile is simple and elegant. The turquoise stripe on a wall of white tile is an inexpensive way to add visual interest to a primarily white bathroom.

LEFT: This sculptural stone bathtub for two at Monteverdi in Tuscany prompts the question of why more tubs don't come in black. In such a dark hue, the tub looks masculine and contemporary and completely commands the room.

OPPOSITE, TOP: While most terraces are furnished with a table and chairs, the Auberge du Soleil focuses one exceptional piece: an oversize stone bathtub. It's placed directly in the center of the space, visible through sliding glass doors, and overlooking a garden— it's impossible to imagine a more beautiful setting for a soak.

OPPOSITE, BELOW: An exceptional bathtub like this claw-foot version with a burnished-metal exterior is rightfully the star of a room at the Singita Ebony Lodge in South Africa.

LEFT: A doorway featuring intricate arches beautifully frames a stunning dark stone tub placed in the center of the room at Amanbagh in Rajasthan, India.

OPPOSITE, TOP: An enormous stone tub with a rounded profile is perfectly framed by floor-to-ceiling windows at the St. Regis in Abu Dhabi. The high-rise location guarantees privacy.

OPPOSITE, BELOW: An ode to marble, this bathroom at The Langham in Chicago features the glamorous material on walls, floors, and ceilings and brings the concept of infinity pools indoors.

A Fresh Take on Tile

White subway tile is a default choice for bathrooms because everyone assumes it's easy and inexpensive. Boutique hotels offer some interesting alternatives, and most won't actually cost more—all that's needed is to think creatively.

Take the cliffside La Minervetta Hotel in Sorrento, Italy. Square, striped tiles are arranged to create horizontal lines on the floor and up the side of the tub. Then the designers simply alternated the tiles, positioning them horizontally and then vertically, along the walls. What could have been a fairly basic striped bathroom instead looks modern and graphic. To make it your own, change the color. A sophisticated city version might be gray and white; for kids, try a vibrant orange or red; for a sunny location, try pink or yellow. The possibilities are truly endless.

Two other examples of how simply reimagining the standard placement of tiles can yield a fresh look come from the Hotel Bachaumont in Paris. In one bathroom, alternating columns of green and white subway tile are placed diagonally rather than horizontally, creating a chevron pattern. It's an attention-grabbing look done on just one wall behind the sink. In another bathroom at the same hotel, designer Dorothée Meilichzon cleverly used sheets of penny tiles, usually relegated to floors, on walls. In the top-floor bathroom, the tiles beautifully catch the light. All of these hotel bathrooms use common and inexpensive bathroom materials, proving that you don't have to spend a lot to get a high-impact look.

OPPOSITE: Rather than using the standard slim white border tile to cap off a lower wall of intricately patterned tile, at Palazzo Margherita in Bernalda, Italy, squares of teal and white with an unusual zigzag design provide a colorful, graphic alternative.

THIS PAGE, ABOVE AND BELOW: By alternating the direction of striped tiles at La Minervetta in Sorrento, Italy, designers have created a cheery, inspired take on basic nautical stripes.

Thin, rectangular tiles in a vivid shade of
blue line walls at Point Yamu by COMO in
Phuket. They are also placed in a square
on the floor as a tub surround. The simple
choice of white mortar makes the tiles look
impressively graphic.

BATHS

TOP: Subway tile, the timeless bathroom staple, is given a fresh twist—literally—when arranged diagonally and in alternating columns of green and white at the Hotel Bachaumont in Paris.

ABOVE: Penny tile is a popular choice for floors, but the inexpensive tile sheets look chic when trimmed with a gold border and coordinating paint on walls at the Hotel Bachaumont in Paris

Pleasing Patterns

Many bathrooms are often smallish spaces, so it really only takes one bold design statement to make an impact. It also sounds counterintuitive, but a small room allows you to get away with using a really strong pattern in a way that would overwhelm a larger space. Especially for bathrooms that don't get a lot of natural light, use pattern to create some visual excitement. At La Minervetta in Sorrento, Italy, for example, wide and alternating red and white horizontal stripes amp up the space and make the small room appear wider.

A second simple way to add pattern to a bathroom is to turn to wallpaper—nothing dictates mood quite as well. Florals can bring in an English country house demeanor while an explosion of graphic patterns can add edginess. At the Tides Beach Club in Kennebunkport, designer Jonathan Adler covered the bathroom walls in a metallic graphic print of blue and silver. At the c/o The Maidstone in East Hampton, designer Jenny Ljungberg injected a staid hotel with bright wallpapers, including a mod floral print by Swedish designer Hanna Werning. The key with intense wallpaper is to pair it with neutral accents and materials.

If you prefer to keep pattern under foot, mosaics and hand-painted tiles add quick flair. Italian hotels are actually a wonderful source of inspiration for tiles—they use brightly colored tile on the floor in a way you don't see as frequently stateside. At the Hotel Capa La Gala in Sorrento, for example, zigzag patterns in orange and blue tile could be re-created not only on bathroom floor, but in a kitchen, mudroom, or foyer.

Another way to introduce pattern is with cement tiles. Some of the most beautiful versions come from Morocco and Mexico. They are expensive, but they hold up well over time and provide an authentically exotic note. The glamorous Sanchaya Estate on Bintan, off Singapore, boasts incredible bathrooms that feature gray-and-white patterned cement tiles. Paired with a pale gray wallpaper, rich woods, marble sinks, and floor-to-ceiling wood-frame mirrors, the effect is sophisticated without being fussy.

Use The Greenwich Hotel in New York as inspiration for overt glamour. An interlocking gray-and-white mosaic pattern of chains covers the floors, and a marble tub and brass fixtures add to the "established" feeling. Exploding the traditional pattern keeps it feeling really fresh. Have the courage to create an intriguing and original design statement.

Cement tiles like these at the Sanchaya on the island of Bintan, off Singapore's southern coast, are an amazing way to bring sophisticated, lasting pattern into a bathroom.

Wallpaper design firm Abnormals Anonymous offers a hipper take on toile—their Meet the Flockers bird print in gray covers bathroom walls at the Palihouse in Santa Monica, California.

At Tides Beach Club in Maine, Jonathan Adler's Syrie graphic and groovy metallic wallpaper and octagonal mirrors are paired with the glamorous marble and nickel Gramercy Double Sink Washstand from Restoration Hardware. Matching up a playful wallpaper with a classic sink design makes the space look fresh.

LEFT: Alternating stone panels flanked with black and white strips of tile creates a sophisticated mood in the Roman Suite at the Palazzo Margherita in Bernalda, Italy.

ABOVE: Red and white stripes instantly bring a sense of fun into a bathroom at La Minervetta in Sorrento, Italy, by riffing on nautical themes.

BELOW: Rather than try to play down the open shower in a small hotel room—a move that always feels like an apology—at The Hoxton in Holborn, they took the less expected choice and made it the focal point of the room by choosing bright-red subway tile.

Luxurious Showers

One feature that will quickly differentiate a luxe property from other hotels is how much square footage they devote to creating roomy bathroom retreats—many are the size of a small bedroom. The bath design gets equal attention as the guest rooms, and features gorgeous materials, beautiful tubs, and high-end fittings and fixtures. Hotel owners also realize that doing something completely unexpected with the bath or shower can make it stand out in the marketplace.

Taking a shower in an unusual or new location or trying out an innovative bath design transforms an everyday task into something much more memorable. Placing a shower outdoors in a garden setting, for example, just can't be beat. At the Amanusa resort in Bali, an al fresco shower springs from a stone wall full of blossoming flowers. Mounting a shower from a ceiling for a rainlike effect is another simple and luxurious touch. It's done beautifully at Dedon Island in the Philippines, where the shower occupies the center of the room—a sunken floor eliminates the need for shower

curtains or walls. It's a fresh take on bathroom design that manages to keep the shower central to the space without overtaking the room. Only on second glance do you even notice it's there.

One of the most unusual showers is at Monteverdi in Tuscany. The showerheads are actually the ends of two curved, metal pipes that arch high into the room. The point? There isn't just one template for shower designs.

OPPOSITE: A shower that emerges from a stone wall laced with blossoms at the Amanusa resort on Bali offers guests an idyllic setting for an outdoor bathing experience and expands ideas about where showerheads can be mounted.

ABOVE: On Dedon Island in the Philippines, a ceiling-mounted shower is placed directly in the center of the room. Thanks to a sunken floor surrounded by a pebble border, no walls or curtains are needed to keep the shower from spraying into the rest of the room.

LEFT: The owners of the Stickett Inn in the Catskills customized a tub from a tractor supply shop to create this unique bathroom. When surrounded by a circular curtain, a ceiling-mounted black showerhead flows into the round, galvanized tub.

OPPOSITE: An unusual shower for two is crafted from high, twin metal pipes that spray water into a wide sunken tub at Monteverdi in Tuscany.

Updating Basic White

White is the safe, obvious, and timeless choice for bathrooms—a key point when you need to think about resale value. It's also easy to design since everything white goes together. There's a reason the look has been a favorite for so long.

But how do you keep an all-white bathroom from feeling unoriginal? As the hotels featured here demonstrate beautifully, there is a way to balance creative design and a white backdrop. At the Whitehall Inn in Maine, for example, the simple choice to add a claw-foot tub in a bright kelly green hue is all that's needed to give the room a fresh spin. One strong shot of color in the otherwise clean, crisp space injects some personality. At the Refinery Hotel in New York, just a small tweak—thin tiles rather than wider, anticipated subway versions, gives a graphic spin to the walls. Paired with a black, marble-topped console sink, brass fittings, and a dark gray pocket door, the hotel shows how just a few small—and inexpensive—details can have a powerful effect on a space.

RIGHT: Everyone knows that pocket doors are huge space savers, but they're also an opportunity for adding color into an otherwise white bathroom. At the Refinery Hotel in New York, the dark gray sliding door also includes a window of tempered glass to help more light travel through the room.

OPPOSITE: A border of black tile mimics the shape and placement of a bath mat at The Ludlow in New York. The hotel's design is meant to evoke a throwback 1980s feel, so they went with the tile shape of the decade—square—for the walls.

FOLLOWING PAGES, TOP LEFT: A tub in a vivid hue—like this kelly green stunner at the Whitehall Inn in Maine—might be all an otherwise-white bathroom needs to feel updated and vivacious.

FOLLOWING PAGES, TOP RIGHT: Simply placing subway tiles in a chevron pattern makes this white bathroom feel way more intriguing. The clawfoot tub in black, rather than the standard white, is another example of a small switch that has a powerful impact.

FOLLOWING PAGES, BOTTOM LEFT: A cement tile floor with a mosaic pattern and a coordinating sage-green tub and cabinet add muted color and pattern to a bathroom with white tile walls at the Vidago Palace in Portugal.

FOLLOWING PAGES, RIGHT: A white aluminum tub at Babylonstoren in South Africa offers a contemporary take on the usual bath. The freestanding Vieques bath from Lavo has sleek lines and the material, when rendered in white, has a modern-meets-rustic vibe.

LEFT: At the Hotel Covell in Los Angeles, slabs of river jade marble bring drama and incredibly gorgeous detail to a compact bathroom. The visually stunning material is a unique choice that commands attention in the space.

OPPOSITE: The Lowell in New York features a breathtaking use of Italian Selene marble with bronze and gray veining—but the overall look still reads as white.

The Bathroom as Oasis

When you shift from thinking about a bathroom as simply a functional space to one that's about relaxing and recharging, your whole perspective on its design changes. Creating a space that feels both calming and beautiful becomes the priority. There are so many ways to create an oasis for yourself based on your personal style and passions. Does a soaking tub with a view inspire serenity? Take cues from the Field Guide in Vermont and place the tub near a window if possible. Take it one step further and find a way to bathe outside? The Amandari outdoor tub surrounded by trees and plants might provide some inspiration. Of course the real-world application would require privacy that could only be guaranteed by a fairly large yard and some distance from the neighbors.

For some, order and minimalist design inspire relaxation. If clutter-free, neutral palettes calm you, take a look at the Aman Tokyo, where an envelope of clean lines and natural materials keep the stress of the bustling city outside away. If you are fairly content with your current bathroom but want to refresh it, bring in a few beautiful and comfortable pieces—ones that aren't really intended for a bathroom at all—to make the space feel warmer. At the J.K. Place Capri, a 1960s style chair is a reminder that a bathroom can be a place to relax for a moment, while at the Borgo Santo Pietro in Tuscany, refined touches like art and an antique chandelier make the space feel incredibly romantic and alluring.

ABOVE: A sunken bathtub is surrounded by trees and greenery in a small courtyard at the Amandari resort in Bali.

OPPOSITE: Monochromatic color can be restful to the eye, even when the color itself is intense. Plaster walls and a tub of blue-green create a restful envelope of pure color at El Fenn in Morocco.

OPPOSITE: At the Aman Tokyo, each room features a *furo*—a deep soaking tub that's traditionally associated with the Japanese ritual of bathing. The pared-down, minimalist aesthetic features classic Japanese materials including camphor wood, washi paper, and stone.

ABOVE: In this bathroom at the Bahia Vik in Uruguay, walls are covered in bamboo instead of the more expected tile for a bathroom that feels like a tropical retreat. By only using one natural material, the overall effect is calming.

LEFT: Adding accessories, furniture, and art that aren't specifically designed for a bathroom adds warmth. At the Borgo Santo Pietro in Tuscany, elegant details like a crystal chandelier, velvet curtains, an intricately carved wood mirror, and framed art create an enchanting retreat.

OPPOSITE, TOP LEFT: Placing the tub underneath a window, like here at the Field Guide in Vermont, maintains privacy while taking advantage of a good view.

OPPOSITE, TOP RIGHT: A bathroom filled with natural materials, such as a ceiling with exposed wood beams, wide stone tiles, and a rustic stone sink reinforces a connection with the natural surroundings at Monteverdi in Tuscany.

OPPOSITE, BELOW: At Mystique in Santorini, a mirror framed in branches dictates the mood of the space, setting an earthy-yet-sophisticated tone.

Masculine Bathrooms

It can be hard to define exactly what makes a space look masculine. The obvious criteria are an absence of flourish and frill and an emphasis on profile and solid-feeling materials. However, it's almost impossible to pinpoint until you see space that immediately conjures up the association. Vertical stripes wrapping the bottom third of the room at both the J.K. Place Roma and the Palazzo Margherita create strong-yet-elegant lines that recall menswear. It also helps that they are created in masculine colors: gray, black, and brown. Small, square mosaic tiles with a strip of color at the Viceroy Central Park in New York have a more urban sensibility, especially when paired with a console sink. Perhaps it is the trend of the moment, but brass fittings also seem to turn up frequently in bathrooms that would be at home in the most James Bond–worthy bachelor pads.

ABOVE: Alternating stripes of gray and white marble, paired with gray paint, at the J.K. Place Roma give this bathroom a tailored, classic feeling.

OPPOSITE: The stripes of this Turkish marble would look equally at home in a bachelor pad as they do at Bahia Vik in Uruguay.

ABOVE: The palette in this bathroom at the Viceroy Central Park in New York—black, gray, white, and dark green—has a masculine feel thanks to its emphasis on straightforward, geometric shapes.

LEFT: At the Central Park in New York, richly patterned marble paired with brass fittings and accessories with an undertone of Art Deco contours is almost as eye-catching as the view.

Alessandra Branca

I travel a tremendous amount, so I feel that hotels can and do inspire every part of our life and design sensibility. I have always liked smaller hotels and prefer those in historic structures, like Chiltern Firehouse and Blakes Hotel in London, and the Italian hotels La Posta Vecchia and Le Sirenuse. Each has left a huge mark on my design references. What most attracts me is a strong cultural identity—they're locally appropriate and wonderfully foreign and familiar all at once.

Favorite Hotel: La Réserve, Paris, France

This is a wonderfully designed *hôtel particulier* on the Right Bank. From the moment you arrive, it feels like an incredibly special and chic residence, and the best part about it is that you never feel you are in a hotel, but rather in the home of a lovely, elegant French family.

Best Space

The private library that only guests can use; it's where I spend many, many hours reading, resting, working, and having tea or a drink. In the winter they light the fireplace and in summer they open the doors open to the wonderful courtyard.

Best Part of the Overall Design

With interiors by the great Jacques Garcia, La Réserve is an updated nod to Napoleon III style, with just the right amount of over-the-top luxe and exoticism mixed in. What I love about this hotel—and frankly most hotels that have a strong, thoroughly defined design—is that you are transported to another time and removed from your everyday life.

Most Unexpected Design Element

The lighting is changed at different times of the day. This is wonderful, and enhances the deep and luxurious jewel tones and the architectural details. There is boiserie, painted and gilt-embossed leather wainscots in the halls, wonderful upholstery, and bronze hardware.

Design Inspirations Brought Home

The rooms on the front of the hotel face the Eiffel Tower, so you get the iconic view that plays off a very calm interior color palette of taupe and gray with a splash of deep red. The bathrooms are incredible—beautifully organized and well lit, with all the amenities you could hope for. The lighting includes hanging lamps in silk and bronze that feel classic yet new.

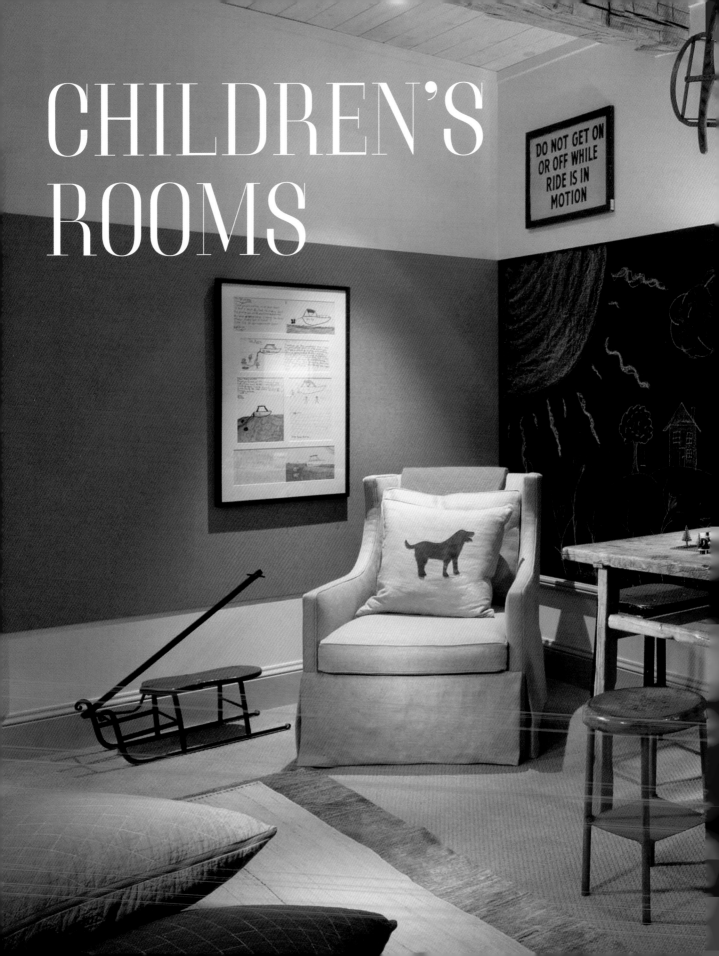

CHILDREN'S ROOMS

DO NOT GET ON
OR OFF WHILE
RIDE IS IN
MOTION

Coloring Outside the Lines

While it is rare to have dedicated rooms or spaces for children at hotels, they are nevertheless full of unexpected design inspiration for little ones. Children's rooms often rely on a confident use of color and pattern to create happy and vibrant spaces. Any hotel that features bold hues, lively prints, fun art, or playful furniture could easily be translated at home in a way that works for kids

Take the seating area at the Avalon Palm Springs, across from the bar. While it definitely is a chic spot for adults to grab a cocktail, it also offers an exciting design template for a playroom: the canary-yellow walls, ceiling, and big mirrors could bring even the darkest room to life. A similar long banquette would be perfect for lots of kids to lounge on while watching a movie. The 1950s-inspired furniture is fun and sturdy enough to handle kids, and a room-length mirror with painted frames could encourage creative art displays.

Colorblocking is another simple design idea that would liven up a children's bedroom, study, or playroom. At the Tides Beach Club in Maine, a suite designed by Jonathan Adler features a room with turquoise walls, except for one painted navy that frames the bed. To make the look your own, just pair two eye-catching colors—orange and royal blue, pink and orange, green and blue—there are endless possibilities.

Another hotel idea great for kids is the inspired use of the ceiling. Take the chalkboard ceilings in the lobby at Mama Shelter in Los Angeles, covered with quirky and colorful drawings. With a little chalkboard paint and some clever positioning—a shoulder perch?—it could be re-created in a playroom and provide an unexpected spot for expressing creativity. Abstract art on the ceiling of a nursery would be great instead of a mobile. Any space with a daring design spirit could serve as inspiration for a child's room.

PREVIOUS PAGES: Two easy ways to foster creativity in a child's room are to incorporate chalkboard paint and corkboard. At Scarp Ridge Lodge in Colorado, two walls provide plenty of space for artwork, drawings, and games.

OPPOSITE: In a bedroom at Maison la Minervetta in Italy, one wall is painted in oversize, horizontal red and white stripes while the facing wall is in navy, in an updated twist on nautical style. A red bed links the two spaces, making the whimsical design feel cohesive.

ABOVE: It's amazing how something as simple as a blanket can completely change the mood of a room. A blue-and-red-striped blanket injects a young, playful spirit into a light-filled bedroom at Maison la Minervetta. Changing bedding can be the simplest way to update a room.

179

LEFT: A sophisticated take on a girly bedroom at the Quirk Hotel in Richmond, Virginia. The designer painted walls in a very pale shade of salmon, then embellished it with upbeat, whimsical art and decorative accessories.

OPPOSITE, TOP: Designer Jonathan Adler playfully pairs navy-painted beadboard with turquoise walls at the Tides Beach Club in Maine, proving that there's no need to limit yourself to just one paint color in a room.

OPPOSITE, BOTTOM: Leave it to designer Kelly Wearstler to make canary yellow both glamorous and cool. Glossy and vibrant yellow walls are paired with a butter-yellow banquette that could adapt to a lounging area. A mirrored wall looks fresh and innovative, and the look would be easy enough to re-create with silver and gold paint. Playful light fixtures and retro furniture complete the fearless and fun space.

LEFT: Painting walls with chalkboard paint is an old trick by now, but why not try the ceiling as they did at Mama Shelter in Los Angeles? It allows endless opportunities for artistic expression that will last longer and are less likely to get smudged accidentally.

OPPOSITE, TOP: The fearless ceilings at Le Royal Monceau-Raffles in Paris should make us all wonder why more places don't use the often-neglected space for colorful abstract art. Imagine re-creating the vibrant design in a baby's room—it's far more exciting than any mobile.

OPPOSITE, BELOW: There's no rule that says art has to be confined by a frame. The Brice in Savannah, Georgia, shows two playful takes on murals. The horse is painted peeking over a fence that extends from the corridor's wainscoting, and dozens of silk butterflies are also tacked to the walls.

CHILDREN'S ROOMS

LEFT: A painted rug is a genius solution for high-traffic rooms like children's bedrooms and play areas. The budget-friendly trick works particularly well in humid or beachside climates, which can be tough on carpets. At the Hotel Escondido in Oaxaca, a graphic pattern gives adds visual punch and a dose of color.

LEFT, BELOW: Dozens of marigolds are painted behind a headboard at Raas DeviGahr in Rajasthan, enlivening an otherwise simple, all-white bedroom.

OPPOSITE, TOP: Designer Vanessa Scoffier gave this bedroom at the Hotel Henriette a graphic hit of navy paint in an unexpected shape. It is a simple, inexpensive, and effortlessly cool idea for transforming a white room. A bonus is that there's no headboard or bedframe required, just paint, pillows, and a chair in a fun shape.

OPPOSITE, BELOW: When you think of a white wall as a blank canvas, it opens up endless possibilities. At the Matachica Resort in Belize, a yellow-and-white abstract design painted on a headboard wall energizes the room.

Bunks

It's pretty much impossible to resist the appeal of a bunk bed. Even kids who aren't fans of going to sleep are eager to experience the high perch of a top bunk or the cozy cocoon of the lower one. Bunks are practical too, since they allow for accommodating more kids. Plus, by stacking beds you're maximizing the floor space—always a plus. Bunk rooms are usually designed for groups of kids, of course, but many hotels and hostels use them to offer inexpensive lodging for adults, too. These spaces can offer design inspiration for making the most of even the smallest quarters. At the Ace Hotel in Portland, Oregon, for example, the clever bunk room layout shows how to make a tiny room into a space for three with an L-shaped configuration.

Hotels provide an abundance of creative design ideas for those who are handy enough to build something rather than go the standard catalog route. The simple bunks at the Field Guide in Vermont are examples of how bunks can be built into a small nook. Scarp Ridge Lodge in Colorado provides a template for how to design a room for five—complete with a triple bunk. At Chalet Pelerin in the French Alps, the bunk design is so chic anyone between the ages of three and a hundred and three would want to spend the night there. Designers Blake Pike and Jane Hines of No. 12 Interiors placed wood slats at the foot of each bed to make the lower beds feel doubly cozy, while providing a built-in ladder to the top.

LEFT: Half the fun of bunk beds is climbing up into them. The topmost bunk at Scarp Ridge Lodge in Crested Butte, Colorado, is accessed via a metal ladder, then a platform, then a short flight of steps..

ABOVE: The bunk room at the Ace Hotel in Portland, Oregon, shows how to make a small room sleep three. The wall also features a collection of band posters that are affixed using wheat paste—a groovy art idea for a teen's room.

OPPOSITE: Two beds in a nook tucked behind a small set of stairs at the Field Guide in Vermont prove how space-efficient bunks can be. Designer Rachel Reider upholstered headboards in plaid and added blankets in a faux-bois pattern for a cozy and cool look.

RIGHT: Wood slats work as ladders while also providing an effect almost like a room screen, separating the beds from the rest of this gorgeous children's room at Chalet Pelerin in the French Alps. The bunk design is rustic-chic, but sheets with lively patterns keep the look young and fresh.

Doubling Up

Whether you are designing a bedroom for siblings or a guest room, it always poses a bigger challenge to create a space for two than for one. Hotels, which often have double beds, offer some solutions for how to make this work visually. Having a uniform backdrop, matching beds, and coordinating bedding helps rid the space of too much visual clutter. Think symmetry—a design trick that works to give the impression of a larger space.

If the idea of a kids' room teeming with color and pattern isn't your thing, take note of the twin rooms at The Dean. The all-white space uses simple beadboard as headboards, then pairs it with sleek lighting and mirrored walls to amp up the crisp, bright space with natural light. All these features make it more intriguing than your basic white box while still retaining the calming, easy qualities of that color.

The twin room at the Hotel Henriette shows that you don't need pricey beds—or even headboards—to make a room intriguing. Instead, mattresses covered in plain white duvets are set against a green headboard wall, but the interesting twist is that the same color wraps the bottom third of the adjacent side walls, to add dimension and structure to the room. Vintage ceiling tiles hung above as art create the illusion of architecture and furniture.

One of the dreamiest children's spaces can be found at Kurland Hotel in South Africa. Their kids' loft features floral sheets and pillows paired with plaid. Bright touches of red and pink in lampshades, pillows, and blankets punctuate the space. The loft also comes with the most personal and fun part of any children's room—toys. Teddy bears, puzzles, and safari animals are ready to play.

This magical children's room at the Kurland Hotel in South Africa features a charming pattern combo of different plaids, florals, and a hit of red on each white bed.

LEFT: Create an energized wall with your child's favorite animal by tracing simple silhouettes on art paper, then affixing them to the wall, as they did at the Peacock Pavilions in Marrakech.

OPPOSITE, TOP: Wood grain blankets, plaid headboards, and feather pillows evoke the rustic, outdoorsy spirit of Vermont at Field Guide. The more grown-up mix of contemporary patterns would be perfect for tweens and up.

OPPOSITE, BELOW: Painting the headboard wall and a third of the side walls in the same soft green endows a small space with a graphic hit, making it feel deliberate and architectural. Vintage ceiling tiles hung as art and two different paper lanterns provide plenty of cool-kid inspiration for a teen's room from the Hotel Henriette in Paris.

CHILDREN'S ROOMS

Playful Patterns

Statement-making patterns featuring interesting motifs and lively colors are perfect for kids' rooms. If you're ready to go bold on walls, take inspiration from the eye-popping, shell-festooned Sunshine wallpaper from Lulu DK at 76 Main on Nantucket. If you prefer a more graphic look, note Vivienne Westwood's Squiggle print for Cole and Son at No. 38, The Park and No. 131 in the Cotswolds. The blue-and-white colorway would be great in a younger child's room, while the orange-and-brown print has a little more of an edge, making it an option for a teen's space.

Themed motifs in children's rooms often get dated quickly when—much as parents dislike admitting it, the child will outgrow his or her favorite animated characters. However, patterns that reflect their passions are a more sophisticated and long-lived option. The bird wallpaper at Field Guide, fish wallpaper at The Attwater, and the book wallpaper at Generator Hostel in Paris all could work beautifully for children who show an interest in those topics.

ABOVE: Eye-catching colors and playful patterns are givens for creating a cheery children's room. At Main on Nantucket, Lulu DK's Sunshine wallpaper—festooned with drawings of sea urchins, coral, and shells—is paired with Christopher Farr's Carnival pillows.

OPPOSITE: Whether you live in Brooklyn or Brussels, you can bring the spirit of the outdoors inside with this A-Twitter wallpaper from Schumacher at the Field Guide in Stowe, Vermont.

OVERLEAF: When choosing a wallpaper for a nursery or young child's room, go with a pattern that they won't age out of too quickly. This whimsical cow and tree print at Suján Rajmahal in Jaipur, India, strikes a good balance between sweet and sophisticated.

OPPOSITE: Designer Kit Kemp often covers walls in fabric rather than wallpaper—it's a trick that instantly makes a room feel softer and cozier. At the Dorset Square Hotel in London, walls are lined in a lively paisley denim with hot pink and white pillows for contrast.

THIS PAGE, TOP AND CENTER: To keep a statement-making wallpaper from feeling too intense in a bedroom, try following a cue from No. 38, The Park, in the Cotswolds and placing it on just on a headboard wall. At the boutique hotel in Gloucestershire, designer and owner Georgie Pearman chose Vivienne Westwood's Squiggle print for Cole and Son.

THIS PAGE, BOTTOM: The ideal wallpaper for bookworms, library wallpaper by Mineheart, gives substance to a simple hostel room at the Generator in Paris.

OPPOSITE, TOP: Although there are four bold prints in this bedroom at The Attwater in Rhode Island, they work seamlessly together because they're linked by a crisp palette of blue, orange, and white.

OPPOSITE, BELOW: At the Hotel Fabric in Paris, brown and white stripes covering one wall are paired with an oversize orange headboard, which provides a lively focal point. Curtains in a happy pink and orange print add some softness to the intense color scheme.

RIGHT: The Attwater in Rhode Island adopts fresh twist on nautical-themed wallpaper—this fish print would work equally well for a kid's bathroom, playroom, or bedroom.

OVERLEAF: All you need is love and groovy décor. At the Hotel Dylan in Woodstock, New York, The Novogratz went with a 1960s-era scheme that would be an inspired design for a teen's room or a basement hangout space. Tapestry wallpaper by Cavern Home offers a graphic backdrop in black and white that lets bright colors like turquoise, yellow, and red stand out even more.

Study Nooks

It goes without saying that creating spaces for children to dream, sleep, and play is the most fun of all—and should be a priority. Incorporating an enjoyable place where they can carve out time for studying, however, might make the school year go more smoothly. Whether they need a place to do algebra or just to draw, creating an appealing study nook where kids want to spend time is key. It can be as simple as upholstering a desk chair in a energetic, vibrant pattern that feels fun—even when homework isn't—like the kilim-covered chair at the Hotel Henriette or the hot pink embossed seats at the Dorset Square Hotel. If space is an issue, try a wall-mounted desk like the designers did at the Hotel Bachaumont. Another space-saving trick? Find a piece that serves multiple purposes, like the desk/bookshelf/cabinet combo at The Hoxton in Amsterdam.

LEFT: Lure kids and teens into doing homework by injecting some levity into spaces that are meant for serious purposes. Homework may not always be fun, but this desk chair upholstered in a vibrant kilim at the Hotel Henriette in Paris definitely is.

ABOVE: A simple black-and-white desk offers a calm contrast to the walls' high-impact, paisley denim pattern at the Dorset Square Hotel in London, while hot-pink chairs embossed with circles provide a cheery perch.

RIGHT: A small built-in desk turns what could have been a forgotten little nook into a functional space at the Palihouse in Santa Monica. A hip take on toile done in a metallic print keeps the look fresh and fun.

LEFT: For budding students, furniture that multitasks is key. A modernist-inspired design at The Hoxton in Amsterdam combines everything a student needs into one piece of furniture: desk, bookshelves, and a closed cabinet.

BELOW: At the Hotel Bachaumont in Paris, a wall-mounted desk provides hidden storage and a work surface without adding bulk to the rest of the room. The compact proportions make it an ideal solution for tight quarters.

OPPOSITE, TOP: This magical space at the Saint James Paris provides plenty of design inspiration. A trompe l'oeil door painted in the manner of Christian Bérard's design for the Institut Guerlain will simply seem whimsical to teens. An enchanting nook complete with a daybed piled high with pillows offers an enchanting hideaway for reading, watching a movie, or just daydreaming.

OPPOSITE, BELOW: An intense shade of blue and a view through an intricately carved window promise to encourage creativity in this work space at El Fenn in Marrakech. The white tulip chair and simple leather-covered desk sit below an art installation by Matt Bryans featuring 221 pieces of sandblasted wood from the ends of discarded Christmas trees.

OVERLEAF: A big, colorful piece of abstract art always has the effect of adding some zing to a room. Designer Patricia Urquiola filled the rooms at the W Hotel in Vieques with pieces that pair function with fun, like the circular Chill Chair—a playful hybrid of chair, lounge, and sofa.

CHILDREN'S ROOMS

Suysel dePedro Cunningham and Anne Maxwell Foster

FOUNDERS OF TILTON FENWICK

Favorite Hotel: c/o The Maidstone Hotel, East Hampton, New York

This hotel epitomizes cozy chic with a bohemian twist. We are especially drawn to the Scandinavian flair and unabashed use of color and pattern.

Best Parts of the Overall Design

We have stayed at the c/o Maidstone in both the peak summer months as well as during the more tranquil winter. In all seasons, the hotel exudes comfort and "Scandinavian cozy." With its white clapboard exterior, manicured lawns, and guests playing board games by the fireplace, it truly feels like a home. The design is quintessentially bold without being jarring. Each of the sixteen rooms and three cottages has its own unique design, and each is dedicated to a Scandinavian celebrity. There is wit and whimsy in every design detail, traits we appreciate and admire.

Best Spaces

We love the common room. Its turquoise walls—Benjamin Moore's Wilmington Spruce—instantly make it the quintessential Hamptons space. A lot of beach hotels favor natural palettes of ivory and sisal for their common rooms, so we appreciate the boldness and pattern in this room.

Intriguing design continues in the "Living Room" restaurant. The black-and-cream floral wallpaper, sage-green molding, and dining chairs covered in black fabric with a primary color pattern somehow work. We pride ourselves in layering pattern upon pattern as designers and being fearless in our interiors, so this restaurant is a perfect example of what we try to attain in our own designs.

Best Parts of the Room

We stayed in the Josef Frank room. His fabrics are used in almost every room in the hotel, but in this particular room, the headboard is a mashup of several of his fabrics. It is a great homage to the famous textile designer and his love of movement and vivid colors. We especially loved the printed fabric on a bedside lampshade and the bathroom wallpaper.

Most Unexpected Design Element

We are huge fans of Alexander Lervik's Lucite-and-LED swing on the front porch. It is an unexpected welcome that conveys the whimsical nature of the c/o Maidstone. It shows that they don't take themselves too seriously and that making your stay fun is paramount.

Design Inspiration Brought Home

Starting small, say with uber-vivid prints on throw pillows, is a good way to get comfortable with the idea of bold color before committing to full-on turquoise walls.

LIBRARIES
AND DENS

A Room for Books

For a book lover, there is nothing quite as glorious as being surrounded by the possibilities of a room full of great reads. Given that vacations are supposed to be ideal times for relaxation, many hotels have begun creating contemporary takes on the library. Some, like the Ham Yard show how a grand, traditional library space can be rendered more modern and accessible; Kit Kemp chose graphic wallpaper and abstract prints. Rather than a chandelier, you'll find sculptural vintage lighting. At the American Trade Hotel in Panama, glossy bookshelves of a deep peacock blue boast bright orange interiors that showcase the shelves' holdings.

Other hotels have come up with clever ways to arrange books. At the Santa Monica, a diamond-grid bookshelf and books placed alternately with spines pointing one way and then the other turns what is essentially storage space into a graphic display. The Brice's floor-to-ceiling open shelves feature neat stacks of colorful tomes lying on their sides, providing a stunning focal point for the room. If you are more likely to download your bestsellers these days but still miss the enchantment of a room teeming with books, The Pig Hotel's charming library wallpaper will be just the trick.

PREVIOUS PAGES: As more people turn to e-books, devoting space to libraries could be becoming a thing of the past. For book lovers, though, nothing beats the look of a room filled with the anticipation of discovering a new author or adventure. If you're an e-book devotee but still consider yourself a bookworm, library-print wallpaper can fill the void. It's available now in prints that show stacks of paperbacks, books arranged by color, and neutral bindings, as shown here at The Pig Hotel in the Cotswolds.

LEFT AND ABOVE: Vintage books crafted with leather bindings and gilded letters will always be appreciated as little works of art in their own right. While most of us don't have such an edited-looking book collection—notice there are no paperbacks in sight—The Hoxton in Amsterdam will inspire you to build your own full of gorgeous, leather-bound classics.

OPPOSITE, TOP:
With high ceilings, lots of light, and inviting floral-print seating, designer Kit Kemp created a particularly inviting library at the Ham Yard Hotel in London. What really makes it unique is the contemporary abstract print on the walls. It's fabric, Christopher Farr's Ozone.

OPPOSITE, BELOW:
There is something unexpected and appealing about displaying books in stacks on their sides. At The Brice in Savannah, Georgia, designer Anna Busta employed thin black shelves for a stunning floor-to-ceiling display of books.

THIS PAGE, TOP:
While inspired by British Colonial style and English country house libraries, designer Kelly Wearstler tweaked the classic, formal formula at the Viceroy Santa Monica. In lieu of a traditional bookshelf, books are graphically displayed in custom diamond cubbies of the sort more usually seen for wine storage. While the furniture style is reminiscent of elegant libraries of old, the wing chairs and a boxy sofa are given a fresh perspective in canary yellow.

THIS PAGE, BOTTOM:
Tropical colors inspire a chic library nook at the American Trade Hotel in Panama. High-gloss bookcases in a rich peacock shade feature the surprise pop of orange backings that highlight the content and form of the shelves' holdings.

Secluded Spaces

Hotels love to wow visitors with grand entry lobbies, but they also know they need to offer guests quieter spots where they can truly unwind, do a little work, or take a phone call. Their ideas for living areas in suites and cozy nooks carved from otherwise unused public spaces are full of ideas for designing a smaller room or den at home. Some, like the Hotel Bachaumont in Paris, play up the teeny proportions they have to work with by incorporating a dark palette for the walls and furniture that feels all-enveloping. Other hotels serve as examples for how to make the most of tight—even awkward—proportions. For example, at the Hotel Jerome in Aspen, a narrow living room is arranged to entertain multiple guests, thanks to a custom, 18-foot-long couch matched with several cocktail tables and well-placed chairs.

As the trend toward constructing enormous living and great rooms continues, ironically the appeal of having a smaller space to use occasionally feels that much more compelling. While larger layouts are wonderful for group gatherings, a cozier, more intimate spot for conversation, reading, working, and lounging feels warm and inviting in a way an oversize space simply doesn't.

Rethink that empty corner in your home by building a bench and piling it high with pillows, enclosing it in dark walls, and lighting it with reading lamps, like at Morocco's Riad Meriem. Try out design moves that are not adaptable to vast settings, like the confident vertical stripes at Singita Sasakwa. Or use power patterns and color to draw your eye away from a room's tight size. At 76 Main on Nantucket, the bold print on a carpet and curtains keeps the focus on the design details, not on the square footage. Whether you are looking for a glamorous den or just to make the most out of a small city living room, hotels yield dozens of innovative ideas—they're experts at making the most out of whatever space is available, and at using every square inch.

To make vintage finds—or just older furniture—look fresh, sometimes all you need is the right backdrop. At the Freehand Hotel in Miami, blue-painted trim warms up a light-filled sunroom and updates the look of the retro furniture.

OPPOSITE, TOP LEFT: Gorgeous colors and sumptuous textures at the Hotel Bachaumont in Paris offer glamorous inspiration for a diminutive seating nook. A deep coral velvet sofa provides comfortable seating in an unusual hue that is echoed in the prints of quirky pouf-stools. A navy carpet with a print that echoes the fan shapes found elsewhere is a complementary color that helps the lighter hues to stand out.

OPPOSITE, TOP RIGHT: The wing chair is a classic piece—and one that's often handed down in families—but making it feel fresh can be a challenge. Designer India Mahdavi came up with a stylish solution for recycling the Connaught's many wing chairs leftover from the London hotel's 2007 renovation. For its Coburg Bar, she gave the vintage chairs a new look by upholstering them in a colorful array of velvets, then trimmed them with a cheeky black fringe.

OPPOSITE, BELOW: Cozy, velvet sofas, Eames Molded Plywood Chairs, rounded ottomans, and circular, low coffee tables that can double as seating offer an abundance of seating options at Altapura in France. The space provides inspiration for how to design a basement hangout space or a kid's playroom.

ABOVE: If you are wondering how maximize space in a long, narrow room, take cues from designer Rachel Reider's design at Main on Nantucket. A path of pattern on the rug and curtains leads your eye to the window and distracts from the tight proportions. Two long sofas are placed on opposite walls, one inset under built-in shelves. Two wing chairs offer even more seating, making the small room work for big groups.

Europeans learned long ago not to fight small spaces,
but to embrace them. At the Hotel Henriette in Paris,
guests in a small seating area are enveloped in a rich
color palette of navy and gray paint, wallpaper, and
furniture. A monochromatic wallpaper like this leaf
version blurs the edges of the tight quarters, while
sculptural lighting and accessories give the eye a
series of interesting objects to rest on and appreciate.

LIBRARIES AND DENS

TOP: At The Buchanan in San Francisco, designed by Nicole Hollis, colorful art hung gallery-style pops against inky blue walls while a long, curved leather couch and velvet armchair entice settling in. The overall emphasis on horizontal visual lines draws the eye down from the low ceilings.

ABOVE: Proving that even the smallest nooks can be put to good use, this gorgeous seating area beckons at the Riad Meriem in Marrakech. The aubergine *tadelakt*, or Moroccan plaster walls, abundance of velvet pillows, and low lighting provide an exotic and enchanting spot for taking in a quiet moment. Designer Thomas Hays chose sculptural accessories to complete the space: an African fish trap as hanging light, a brass French table lamp, and a juju hat from Cameroon hung as art.

ABOVE: A few well-chosen details make a huge impact in smaller spaces. Sheepskin throws, a Moroccan pendant lamp, and abstract printed curtains all help create The Ludlow's seemingly effortless brand of cool in this diminutive sunroom.

OPPOSITE, ABOVE: This Colonial-inspired space at the Singita Sasakwa makes a great jumping-off point for the unexpected design of a somewhat formal home den. The striped walls could be customized to suit your style or existing accessories. For example, gray and white stripes would set a sophisticated tone, while yellow and white would create a more cheerful backdrop.

OPPOSITE, BELOW: This suite at the Hotel Jerome in Aspen is ready for cocktails. A variety of tables and chairs set across from an 18-foot-long couch provide plenty of spots for conversation, games, and drinks from the suite's in-house bar. Replace the little tables with a long one, and you'd have a dining area that could suit large groups.

Mary McDonald

Favorite Hotel: L'Hotel, Paris, France

I could never choose just one hotel as a favorite since my tastes run the gamut—the design elements of quite a few imprinted in my mind for various reasons. I love The Umaid Bhawan palace in Jodhpur for its unrivaled Raj style and elegant glamour, and The Palais Jamai in Fez for old-school Moroccan tiled elegance and whimsy. Also the Hotel Il San Pietro in Positano for a lesson in Italian style complete with colorfully tiled benches, baths, and floors and gilded headboards and colorful, zesty Italianate interiors celebrating the Amalfi coast. I can say, though that L'Hotel in Paris is one I return to again and again. I like that it is not trying to be modern. It celebrates historic French style.

Best Parts of the Overall Design

I am drawn to almost everything Jacques Garcia designs. He achieves a level of layering you would usually only find in an authentic French home or *hôtel particulier*. At L'Hotel, the antique sconces, the artful use of stripes on stripes dove tailing with pattern, and punctuating trim and details are something only the French pull off this well.

Best Space

The circular stairwell that wraps the downstairs vestibule. It has a glamorous, tricolored marble patterned floor. It interjects a sense of history, architecture, and old-world glamour. You would want this in your home if you could have it.

Best Parts of the Room

L'Hotel manages to make me feel French—very, very French. How? Because of the way they make it feel so personal. Surprisingly, all the rooms are all different, and all in perfect taste. Each is furnished with its own set of antiques, from the expected Directoire chairs to over-the-top mirrors. Some rooms have one whimsical piece, such as a huge, overscaled nineteenth-century carved mirror over a plump bed that's hard to resist. Other rooms seduce with rather Malmaison-esque detailed trim in two tones and stripes adorning the a quintessentially French headboard. Lighting achieves mood perfectly, like they know what you need better than you do yourself.

Most Unexpected Design Detail

The pool in the basement, which reads like something carved out of an eighteenth-century wine cellar.

Design Inspirations Brought Home

The intricate layering of French historical decorative art references, like the fully upholstered tables and console pieces, the detailed and classic trompe l'oeil scenes with upholstered walls, and the use of double curtains throughout.

Foyers

They say it's all in the details, and that is definitely true when it comes to design—especially of foyers. Unlike a home, which is usually added to over time, every detail of a hotel room is thought out in advance. Designers think of how each item will work together to create an overall feeling for a space. Whether they are creating an entry environment that is meant to feel Zen or seductive or glamorous—everything from paintings to sconces to floor tile is a well-chosen part of a larger vision. It makes hotels a unique source of inspiration for residential interiors; look at your own spaces with a view to understanding how each small thing impacts the way a room feels.

For many, a foyer is simply a functional place to drop your keys. It's often default-decorated with a circular central table in a larger space, or two chairs and a high table in a tighter quarters. Although it is essentially a pass-through, why not take some cues from hotel design? The coolest properties use entrances as opportunities to dazzle arriving guests.

One way to make an immediate impact in an entrance is with wallpaper. The Suján Rajmahal provides a spectacular example of how vivid colors and lively pattern can draw you into a space. Stepping into a space festooned with pattern is an incredible way to transition from the outside in, and

since foyers are usually smallish spaces you can get away with a small dose of a big, bold print. Foyers at home often include a pair of chairs that no one really uses. Why not shake it up with a pair of chairs that make a powerful visual statement—people might actually use them. The porter chairs at the Grace Bay Club and the retro-inspired pair at the Oceana Beach Club have sculptural lines and spectacular curves. They entice you to sit and make the space your own, if only for a minute.

PREVIOUS PAGES: Framed pictures of Lord Srinath Ji with his different *darshans* are hung in multiples and arranged by color at the Raas DeviGarh in India. The graphic arrangement could be re-created with any favorite motif or series of prints to enliven a wall.

OPPOSITE: Bespoke wallpapers designed by Adil Ahmad and produced by Good Earth for the Suján Rajmahal Palace were inspired by the traditional motifs and colors of the royal family of Jaipur. This floral-festooned, cypress-tree design features richly saturated colors and patterns. A bright or bold pattern is an easy way to enliven a space.

ABOVE: An empty corner can be transformed from a wasted space into a welcoming seating nook, as the Jnane Tamsna in Morocco shows. The combination of two hand-carved settees, potted plants, flat-weave carpets, and identical framed mirrors arranged in a grid gives this former byway new life.

OPPOSITE, TOP: The classic foyer pairing of an entry table and two chairs gets a fresh spin at the Oceana Beach Club Hotel in Santa Monica, California. Designer Anthony Baratta custom designed these exaggerated takes on wing chairs that make the space feel like somewhere you could actually have fun, rather than just somewhere to drop bags after a busy day.

OPPOSITE, BELOW: In sixteenth-century France, canopied chairs provided a perch for porters who greeted—or turned away—guests at the entrances to grand homes. At the Grace Bay Club in Turks and Caicos, designer Thom Filicia placed an updated take on porter chairs in the lobby in a nod to their original use.

RIGHT: An assortment of *objets*, sculptures, vessels, books, and art form an intriguing display around a bookshelf at the Siam Hotel in Bangkok, designed by Bill Bensley. A muted palette unites the individual pieces into one cohesive grouping.

Lighting

Lighting is the jewelry of a room. It adds a little shimmer, a hit of sparkle, a pop of color, or a sculptural touch—all while casting a gorgeous glow. The material of a lighting fixture can set the tone for an entire room. A hint of brass evokes retro or nautical style, crystal conjures a romantic mood, Lucite has a playful feel, iron has a more masculine edge, and colorful ceramics bring in some levity. With retro design being a huge trend in hotel design at the moment, you'll start noticing bronze light fixtures that echo vintage design virtually everywhere. At The Chequit on Shelter Island, designer Kevin O'Shea chose hand-rubbed brass sconces for bedside lighting. The delicate, antique-inspired design complements the hotel's Victorian-era and nautical roots while the silhouette makes them feel fresh.

After style, the most important aspect of a lighting fixture is the type of light it emits. Overly bright spaces can feel clinical or institutional. Overly dark spaces can feel sinister. However, when it is just right, lighting can dictate the mood of the room. At the Siam Hotel in Bangkok, small cast-iron lanterns provide a subtle glow that feels calming and cozy. At the C.O.Q. in Paris, two globe lights and two tiny reading lights conjure an alluring vibe in dark-hued rooms—anything brighter would kill the mood.

Lighting is one of the most often overlooked details in a home. By examining how lighting is given its own prominence and presence in hotels, you can see how it underscores a space's style. Creating beautiful lighting treatments is truly an art—pieces can almost double as sculpture. Case in point: the glamorous vintage sconces at the Hotel Henriette in Paris. Eight leaves extend from the wall, arching over glowing bulbs while casting a seductive, glamorous spell. It's a reminder that while lighting is of course a practical need, the best lighting can bring flair and glamour into a space.

LEFT, ABOVE: A vintage sconce in brass, shaped like leaves that curl around individual bulbs, casts an understatedly glamorous glow at the Hotel Henriette in Paris. The leaf design also echoes the foliage pattern on the wallpaper.

LEFT: At the Ace Hotel Downtown Los Angeles, the bed's headboard also functions as a desk—a smart space-saving solution for smaller rooms. The lighting, custom-designed by Atelier de Troupe, also serves dual purposes and can be positioned to spotlight either the bed or desk.

OPPOSITE: Lanterns are usually used outdoors, but at the Siam Hotel in Bangkok, small, cast-iron wall lanterns in a traditional shape offer an unexpected take on bedside lighting.

OPPOSITE, TOP: Lighting is kept subtle and low at the C.O.Q. hotel in Paris. Built-in positionable reading lights flank the bed while a shelf provides a perch for luminous globes.

OPPOSITE, BOTTOM LEFT: At the Chequit on Shelter Island, delicate and refined wall-mounted light fixtures in brass have a vintage look that acknowledges the property's Victorian-era roots.

OPPOSITE, BOTTOM RIGHT: At Locanda Al Colle guest house in Italy, a 1950s sconce fits in beautifully with a room full of midcentury furniture.

ABOVE: Half-globe brass wall sconces line an innovative, colorblocked hallway at The Hoxton in Amsterdam.

BELOW: Small, round spotlights and a lighting strip underneath a shelf at the Sixty SoHo in New York gives a mirrored bar a warm glow.

RIGHT: The line between lighting and sculpture is blurred with this striking three-pronged lamp at The Hoxton in Amsterdam.

Dramatic Walls and Floors

Hotels love to wow. Statement floors and pattern-festooned walls do just that. Going bold with a backdrop is a way to immediately energize a space. It's also a design slight of hand that can be used by the rest of us. High-impact floors and walls distract from a room's drawbacks—lack of light, odd proportions, or narrow confines. The attention goes to the daring design, not the space's limitations.

One of the most fearless floors can be found at Capo La Gala in Sorrento, Italy. Navy and white zigzag floors in glossy tile set a lively tone, yet somehow the move feels comfortably classic. How could you not have fun in that hotel? That same pattern could of course be translated in endless colorways, and would be a cheery choice to rev up any dark room—think kitchens, mudrooms, or bathrooms.

Flooring, whether bold or subtle, makes a design statement. Walk into a suite at the Viceroy Central Park in New York, and of course your eye will be drawn to the casement windows with incredible city and park views—but the rich wood floors in a herringbone pattern are one of the interiors' most dazzling features. The floors add a graphic element to the room that's impossible to ignore. Imagine if

design firm AvroKO had gone with carpet—it simply wouldn't have had the same impact. One detail can be crucial, and flooring is often the punctuating element.

Hallways are wonderful opportunities to be more adventurous with your design choices. The Suján Rajmahal in India provides an exquisite lesson about not letting any surface go untouched. The floors in a hall are done in cream and orange tiles, arranged in a checkerboard; the ceilings are painted a bright shade of poppy; and the walls are covered in a custom floral-and-bird print paper in a blue, red, and pink. Each archway is lined with mirrors to reflect and magnify the glorious colors and patterns. It's a reminder that no space is too practical to celebrate with exuberance, and that even a hallway can become something magical.

OPPOSITE: An exquisite mosaic tile floor that surrounds a fountain in a courtyard at the La Sultana in Marrakech provides many individual motifs that could be extracted and re-created at home in a simpler arrangement.

ABOVE: In a high-traffic area or mudroom, consider lining the lower half of a wall with tile instead of painted wainscoting that will inevitably get scuffed up, as they did at The Hoxton in Amsterdam.

LEFT: The floor at the Sixty SoHo features a graphic pattern in the same sophisticated color palette as the overall design. Investing this much attention on a floor means other furnishings can be kept minimal. These cement tiles were custom designed by Tara Bernerd & Partners and crafted by Mosaic del Sur.

LEFT, BELOW: There's no need for carpets with rich wood floors like these. In an update on herringbone, the subtle variation between individual boards adds depth at the Viceroy Central Park in New York City.

OPPOSITE, ABOVE: In Italy, tile is often used throughout the house, not just in bathrooms and in kitchens. At Capo La Gala, sky-blue tiles set in a herringbone pattern bring some pizazz to a living room and bedroom that carpet could never replicate.

OPPOSITE, BELOW: Navy and white tiles set in a zigzag pattern make a high-impact statement in the lobby of Capo La Gala in Sorrento, Italy. The treatment would look equally captivating at home in a bathroom, mudroom, or kitchen.

PREVIOUS PAGES, LEFT: Nothing enlivens a long, dark hallway like wallpaper in a vibrant pattern. At the Hotel Palisade in Sydney, a show-stopping marbleized paper is paired with black-and-white diamond floors.

PREVIOUS PAGES, TOP RIGHT: A dazzling display of color and pattern proves that more is more at the Suján Rajmahal in India. Orange checkerboard floors, poppy-hued ceilings, and red velvet sofas echo the vivid hues found in a lively floral-and-bird wallpaper. The effect is amplified by mirrored archways.

PREVIOUS PAGES, RIGHT BOTTOM: At Vidago Palace in Portugal, a tropical landscape wallpaper brings the outdoors into a long, narrow hallway. As muralists and designers have known for centuries, scenic wallpaper is one of the most effective ways to expand the confines of an interior space.

OPPOSITE: This walk-in closet at La Mamounia in Marrakech is a reminder that even the most utilitarian spaces can be transformed into something magical. This navy closet features hand-painted tiles, hand-carved trim, and Moorish archways.

RIGHT, ABOVE: At the Viceroy Santa Monica, crisp gray-and-white-striped carpet placed horizontally in the bedroom and vertically in the living room both links and delineates the two spaces.

RIGHT, BELOW: Hand-painted concrete tiles are a staple of Mexican design. At The Cape in Los Cabos, tiles are rendered in a palette that is at once earthy and urbane. While patterned tiles are a gorgeous way to add pattern, they can literally feel cold, so to warm up the space designer Marisabel Gómez Vázquez placed a sisal carpet around the bed.

Setting the Tone with Art

Art is so personal. It can inspire, provoke, or transport. We've all been to hotels where clichéd landscapes rule the hallways, and paint-by-number prints fill the bedrooms. However, in hotels that are designed to feel personal, as if you are staying in the home of a very cool friend, the art also reflects that sensibility. Designers are throwing out the idea that they need to hang paintings that will appeal to all in spaces that will be used by many and are filling the walls with one-of-a-kind pieces instead.

Take The Buchanan in San Francisco, where paintings by local artists are assembled gallery-style in the lobby. Each piece pops against dark blue-green walls, their colors rendered more intense against the backdrop. While at least two of the pieces have tongue-in-cheek references to more famous pieces—the *Girl with a Pearl Earring* looks like she is standing in a bar, and a diner looks like a miniature version of *Nighthawks* by Edward Hopper—neither looks either expensive or overly curated. Instead, they look like a grouping you could put together from flea market finds. There is something so charming about seeing that type of arrangement at a hotel, in place of something more grand or pricey.

Art also adds depth and a point of view. At the Continentale in Florence, a black-and-white montage photograph by Faye Heller echoes—or perhaps leads—the retro 1950s-inspired design because it recalls movie stills of the era. It's easy to imagine that the lobby seating area, with its hot pink and black vintage-inspired chairs and the Audrey Hepburn movies playing on the TVs, could have taken its design cues from the art.

A great, easy, and replicable art idea comes from the Palihotel in West Hollywood. Dozens of Polaroids of the neighborhood—many that are close-ups or abstract images—were arranged in a grid, matted, and hung in oversize white frames. It looks like one cohesive piece from a distance and is equally intriguing when examined, since it has so many links to the local area. What a fun project to try

Red walls provide a stunning backdrop for an intriguing collection of art, mostly rendered in black and white for the Baccarat Hotel in New York. While this was assembled by curators Stéphanie and Frédéric Chambre, a quick study of the various types of art that are mixed together here—contemporary portraits, vintage photos, and abstract line art—reveal pieces that could go into an equally cohesive-looking gallery wall at home

OPPOSITE: At Le Royal Monceau-Raffles in Paris, designer Philippe Starck placed an oversize work of art on the floor, leaning against the wall. This is a casual and unexpected way to display art. It also works beautifully when paired with a sculptural piece of furniture to create a striking vignette.

RIGHT, ABOVE: The design of the glamorous Dior Suite at the St. Regis in New York was inspired by the brand's Paris atelier. Walls and upholstery are finished in "Dior Gray" and paired with Louis XV–style seating placed throughout. Artist Bil Donovan's watercolor tribute to Dior's fashion designs completes the chic space and subtly underscores the theme. Consider incorporating art that subtly pairs with a room's mood or prevailing aesthetic.

RIGHT, BELOW: Black-and-white montage photographs by artist Faye Heller are paired with retro-inspired chairs in a black, white, and pink palette to create a 1950s, Audrey Hepburn–inspired space at the Continentale in Florence.

ABOVE AND BELOW: While white walls are the favorite backdrop of many museums and galleries, dark walls can make art appear more vibrant. In The Buchanan lobby, designed by Nicole Hollis, small-scale oil paintings by local artists pop against teal walls. Abstract art inspired by details extracted from Japanese patterns also punctuates a bedroom space in the same hotel. It's an example of how even small pieces can set the tone for a room.

RIGHT, BELOW: Classic brass picture lights add gravitas to any work of art. At the Hotel Providence in Paris, they spotlight two framed artworks while contemporary furniture keeps the room, which also features traditional dentil molding, looking chic.

At the Palihotel in West Hollywood, framed Polaroids taken of the immediate neighborhood, arranged in an oversized grid and matted in an outsize picture frame, create a very fresh piece of original art that gives the room a sense of place and would be easy to re-create in any location.

Michele Bonan

Favorite Hotels:
Claridge's, London, and
The Carlyle, New York

I love the look and feeling of a classic, grand hotel. Both these hotels have that classic background and a timeless atmosphere mixed with great service. Claridge's is a masterpiece favored by royalty, and is a symbol of British style. The Carlyle is an embodiment of Madison Avenue style that exudes luxury, elegance, and refinement.

Best Parts of the Overall Design

The Claridge's entrance and its revolving door is a Deco landmark and trademark of the hotel. I love the graphic elements. The floors have the same graphic effect, though they tend toward the classic. The way they match with the Deco elements makes them unique.

At The Carlyle, I like the emphasis on symmetry and the large windows with views of Central Park.

Best Spaces

At Claridge's I am most drawn to the tearoom because it has a classic feel that adapts its atmosphere to each moment of the day. From morning through teatime to dinner, it adapts to the mood of the moment. It could only be thanks to the special off-white color.

At The Carlyle, I love Bemelman's Bar because it has a wonderful atmosphere that's at once cozy and full of New York energy—this balance makes it special. All the dining spaces at The Carlyle, in fact, have a special atmosphere that feels private, glamorous, and romantic, while Claridge's has the allure of classic English style.

Design Inspiration Brought Home:

I am constantly inspired by what surrounds me—not only by what I see, but even by what I feel or hear. The elegance of both these hotels have inspired my own hotel designs. These hotels have a classic, homey feeling as well as character. The service pays special attention to each guest without being too invasive. You can feel at home and feel the city vibe, too.

OUTDOOR
SPACES

Terraces and Rooftops

One of the most sought-after spaces in any city is a terrace or roof deck. Perhaps because they're in the midst of an urban setting, even small outdoor spaces feels like a true luxury. Add in beckoning seating, a variety of plants, soft lighting, twinkling city buildings or starry skies, and these al fresco spaces can become truly magical.

The Sixty SoHo in New York provides a great example of how to create an enchanting escape. Standard-issue concrete floors feature painted baby-blue triangles, creating a cheery take on an outdoor rug, and sectional seating is upholstered simply but in vibrant blues and yellows that adds instant punch against the predominantly brick-and-gray skyline. The rest of the furniture is easy and weatherproof. Circular coffee tables, fun squatty wicker stools, and a marble dining table are paired with a couple of interesting iron-mesh chairs. Exposed party lights are strung overhead. A variety of potted trees, including evergreen firs, surround the seating to give guests some privacy as well as a feeling of being buffered from the city. Because all different types of plants cohabit, the space doesn't feel too precious or manicured, just like it was assembled off the cuff—and that effortless sensibility adds to its appeal even more.

PREVIOUS PAGES: A daybed set up in a corner, with crisp white cushions and pillows like this one at the Uxua Casa Hotel & Spa in Brazil, would create an alluring retreat that encourages you to put your feet up. Plus, it's big enough to share.

OPPOSITE: At Sixty SoHo, a bright-blue sectional, yellow pillows, and baby-blue triangles painted on plain concrete tiles add a playful spirit to a rooftop oasis in the middle of downtown Manhattan.

THIS PAGE: Black and white stripes are in keeping with the posh, tailored décor at London's glamorous and storied Connaught in Mayfair.

OPPOSITE, TOP: The roof at Le Sirenuse in Positano, Italy, features a cheerful Mediterranean palette of canary yellow, royal blue, and crisp white that complements the stunning blues of sea and sky. The color combo would brighten dreary gray city days or add punch to a verdant backdrop anywhere. Painting faded garden ornaments or fountains a bright hue will help make them look more current.

OPPOSITE, BOTTOM: Inspiration for designing a contemporary and minimalist outdoor space abounds at The Cape in Los Cabos. This sleek outdoor space's design hinges on just three basic features: floor tiles in a gray-and-white abstract pattern, a boxy side table, and stunning sculptural chairs.

THIS PAGE, TOP: At the Hotel Azúcar in Mexico, a rustic wooden pergola was built with slight gaps, to let just enough sunlight in while still providing shade on a rooftop terrace. It also works perfectly for hanging a hammock. A few simple pink cushions of different shapes form an easy, ground-level lounging area.

THIS PAGE, BOTTOM: A *palapa* typical of the Yucatán provides shade at Casa Las Tortugas on Isla Holbox in Mexico. The rustic-chic design offers a sculptural, almost graphic take on a canopy. It is definitely a cooler alternative to the standard patio umbrella.

Courtyards and Solariums

Since courtyards and atriums are a hybrid of indoor and outdoor, they are full of design ideas that can be used in a wide range of spaces. For example: the tile floors that show up so frequently in courtyards due to their durability. These are also smart choices for other high-traffic areas that might see dirty shoes, water, or the occasional spill—mudrooms, covered porches, kitchens, bathrooms, and small conservatories or sunrooms. The atriums at The Hoxton in Amsterdam and the Saint James and Hotel Henriette in Paris showcase a wide range of design possibilities for tile.

Although it's renowned for its practicality, tile can also look quite glamorous, especially when combined with vintage furniture and a gorgeous backdrop. The intricate floral tile floors in the winter garden at the Saint James in Paris give the space a layered feeling, punctuating the room with an ornate pattern that feels imported from another, more genteel, era. A modern, playful take on a tile floor can be found at

The Hoxton in Amsterdam. There, a seemingly random mix of blue, gray, navy, and white square tiles cast fresh, energetic spirit over the whole space. That tile pattern carries over from the kitchen next door, and it's a fresh look that would fit equally well in a playroom, too. The Hotel Henriette features a gray-and-white cement tile floor in a gorgeous pattern that would look just as chic in a bathroom or foyer. That space proves how a bold patterned floor can take the lead in a room.

OPPOSITE: The glass-enclosed *jardin d'hiver*, or winter garden, at the Hotel Henriette in Paris features a stunning tile floor. It's the only embellishment the glass-enclosed space overlooking the garden really requires.

ABOVE: A glass-fronted cabinet, a bust tucked under a table, and throw blankets and pillows bring warmth and personality to a glass-enclosed living space at Ett Hem in Stockholm. Solariums filled with comfortable furniture and plants always get plenty of use in colder or gray climates, but it's rare for them to feel as current.

OPPOSITE, TOP AND BOTTOM: Whether set aglow with lanterns at night or adorned with a hammock tied between two trees during the day, an interior courtyard always feels like a secret indulgence. At El Fenn in Marrakech, low orange sofas stacked with colorful throw pillows, in-ground trees, a checkerboard floor, and hand-carved doors are just a few of the details that could be re-created in any warm climate to evoke more exotic locations.

ABOVE: Mix china you inherited with a few basic white chargers from a big-box store, and voilà, a graphic arrangement of plates for any patio. At the Viceroy Santa Monica, a symmetrical design pops against a dark wall. Another unexpected move is bringing traditionally indoor furniture, like wing chairs, outdoors. It could work for any warm, dry climate to make an al fresco space feel cozier and warmer than wood or wicker chairs would.

Simple shelves and steps filled with a random collection of blooming terra-cotta pots, plus a lively patchwork of blue, gray, and white basic square floor tiles are all that's needed to make a small, sun-drenched solarium like this one at The Hoxton in Amsterdam feel festive.

A mural depicting ivy echoes live greenery in a winter garden on the top floor at the Saint James in Paris. Red velvet curtains, elaborate floor tiles, mirrored glass windows, and a vintage porter chair complete the space..

Porches

Porches offer the best of everything: covered above, they're protected from the elements; open on three sides, they connect us to the outdoors. There is also more freedom in designing porches than other al fresco spaces whose traditional purposes are usually more defined. Materials you would normally think of as indoor options can be used here—even art can make an appearance—blurring the lines further between indoor and outdoor living.

The porches on display here span the style spectrum. If you live in a traditional home, take a style cue from The Chequit on Shelter Island. The Victorian-era hotel features a porch filled with pieces that you might have inherited from your grandmother—Windsor chairs and white wicker sofas. Crisp gray cushions, raw-edged wood slab tables, and abstract printed carpets give the space a fresh twist, however.

If trying to re-create a glamorous escapade in an exotic location, look to the Raas DeviGarh in India: colorful daybeds feature bright silk bolsters, metallic embroidered pillows liven up chairs, glossy black-and-white floors in bold patterns create a copia of zing, and a wall of identical lanterns casts beguiling light. To feel happy tropical vibes anywhere in the world, try the Cotton House Resort's combination of lively purple-and-white prints and salmon-colored pillows. If your dream is a sophisticated-yet-serene retreat—and you are someone who is not prone to spills—imitate the Sanchaya Estate's arrangement of all-white cushions and top them off with a black-and-white awning.

OPPOSITE: A covered outdoor space can be layered with as much detail as an indoor room. At the Peacock Pavilions in Marrakech, designer Maryam Montague covered cushions in custom wool-and-sequin Moroccan wedding blankets, while vintage Beni Ouarain and Azilal carpets are layered on the ground. Montague made the tables out of antique Fez tea trays from the 1940s, and pendant lanterns that double as hanging sculpture provide lighting.

ABOVE: The unusual color pairing of green and peach instantly sets a glamorous Jacques Garcia-designed porch apart at La Mamounia in Marrakech. Add in the trellis canopy, floor tiles, and a mosaic tile bench—all three of which feature different diamond grid motif—and the result is an intricately patterned and layered, one-of-a-kind haven that shows enticingly how the light shifts throughout the day.

The Singita Mara River Tented Camp in Tanzania is so carefully outfitted, it's difficult to believe that it's actually not a permanent space. The boxy wrap-around sofa, grouping of sculptural tables, pendant lights, and natural materials would create a sophisticated safari look in any city apartment.

TOP: Black-and-white shades, patterned tile floors, well-crafted teak furniture, and crisp white cushions offer a sophisticated take on exotic style at the Sanchaya Bintan Estate, off the coast of Singapore.

ABOVE: At the Colony Palms Hotel in Palm Springs, touches of red unify the draped, cozy space—they appear in the fabric's stripes, on piping, and in the floor tiles. One signature color can work to unify a porch filled with items with different provenances.

LEFT: A sectional sofa maximizes seating in a small space. At the Cotton House, on Mustique, a colorful array of pillows adds personality to the classic, boxy white sectional without distracting from the porch's real appeal: the setting amid an abundance of tropical greenery.

BELOW: Furniture that is low to the ground gives off a relaxed, unfussy vibe. At the Uxua Casa Hotel & Spa in Brazil, low tables, long cushions, and woven mats furnish a mellow, shaded outdoor lounge area. A similar nook could be created in a home yard, and keeping the color scheme to all white would inject it with a beachside serenity.

RIGHT: Benches built between posts are a clever way to incorporate seating, as they did for this open-air room at Uxua Casa Hotel & Spa in Brazil. The easy seating is made more comfortable with rectangular white cushions and stacked pillows.

Outdoor Dining

On vacation, dinner just might include a view that you've journeyed hundreds of miles to see. But even if you don't have quite the same scenic vistas at home, you can still can still glean inspiration from outdoor dining spots from around the globe.

One of the most glamorous and inventive ideas is courtesy of the Viceroy Santa Monica, where a black-and-white cabana has been transformed into an outdoor dining room. A few sophisticated details usually reserved for indoor dining—a white tablecloth and a hanging mirror—have been brought outdoors. Both hanging and floor lanterns team up with candelabras and votives to give off an ethereal glow. A cabana is a clever and unexpected way to add an outdoor dining space, with the extra bonus of protecting diners from a passing shower. While cabanas are usually set up poolside, if anchored properly one could be set up on a rooftop or in a backyard with a table and chairs. Even if it's not quite as elaborate as this version, it will provide a lovely spot to relish an outdoor meal.

While tables for two are common in restaurants, at home the instinct is to only buy tables that have room to seat the whole family. However, there is something simple and romantic about just having a dedicated space for a couple. At the Borgo Santo Pietro in Tuscany, for example, a painted wrought-iron table and chairs are set up in a corner of a garden, and that's all that's needed to create a dreamy spot for morning coffee, a quick snack, a place to read with a cup of tea, or maybe a game of checkers. Reevaluate your own backyard for an underused space where a small dining set could go.

ABOVE: Sometimes table settings are all that's needed to transport us back to vacation for a little while. At the Avalon in Palm Springs, a neutral gray banquette instantly takes on tropical flair when paired with a modern white table and chairs, a tie-dye runner, potted plants, and exotic-print throw pillows.

RIGHT: A patina of age on any vintage or flea market French bistro set always adds to its charm, as the designers of the Hotel Henriette in Paris know well.

OPPOSITE, TOP: While this space at Raas DeviGarh in Rajasthan, India, could technically accommodate a larger table, fitting it with one that only has room for two makes the already romantic porch and vista seem even more so.

OPPOSITE, BELOW: Setting up a small table and chairs in an out-of-the-way corner of a backyard or garden creates an incredibly romantic spot. A vintage wrought-iron table and chair set in the corner of a beautifully landscaped garden at the Borgo Santo Pietro in Tuscany is a perfect example.

THIS PAGE, RIGHT: The classic pairing of navy and white often conjures up nautical scenes. At the Malliouhana in Anguilla, for example, blue-and-white-striped pillows set on white wicker armchairs provide a comfortable perch to enjoy a meal with a view. Embrace any view you may have of a body of water by creating an equally crisp and tailored setting for meals so you'll encourage yourself to take advantage of it.

THIS PAGE, BOTTOM: While cabanas are traditionally used as poolside shields from the sun, at the Viceroy Santa Monica Kelly Wearstler reappropriated them as private, outdoor dining rooms. A mirror and hanging lanterns add homey touches usually reserved for interior spaces, while candlelight creates a dreamy glow. Creating a humbler version at home would provide an alluring new space for dinner parties.

Poolsides

Pool designs have evolved to take on as much personality and style as any other space. Now even your pool can reflect your personality. If you want to conjure old Hollywood glam at home, try taking a page from the Avalon Palm Springs, which features black-and-white, classic cabanas and bright yellow lounge cushions. If you love the look of cabanas but want your poolside to feel more fun, keep the yellow lounge chairs, but pick out cabanas in bold stripes and lively hues, like the ones at the Thompson Miami Beach.

If you want to create a more exotic, tropical feeling, layer colorful woven carpets around the perimeter of your pool. It softens the look of stone or brick, and makes the space look both more festive and glamorous. It's a fun choice if you are throwing a party poolside. Another unexpected idea is to say farewell to standard lounge chairs and to adopt placing cushions directly on the ground around the pool. In a bright shade like the hot pink, at shown at the Azúcar, it adds punch and verve while also creating a relaxed, bohemian vibe.

Don't always default to lounge chairs—bright pink and plaid cushions set on low platforms or directly on the ground at the Azúcar in Mexico are fun, relaxed, and less expensive.

The Nihiwatu in Indonesia takes
poolside dining to the extreme:
benches and a table hover just above
the surface of the pool.

OUTDOOR SPACES

Whether set on a beach or poolside, a *palapa* or tiki hut will always create an exotic and tropical mood. At the Four Seasons on Koh Samui, sunken seating and an S-shaped bar provide a glorious retreat with a view. Construct a smaller version at home or even group several grass patio umbrellas together to inject a tropical vibe.

LEFT: If you need inspiration for forgoing standard white for cabanas, beach umbrellas, or loungers, take a look at what bold stripes, turquoise fabric, and yellow lounge chairs can do. At the Thompson Miami Beach, the playful color combination instantly inspires a festive mood.

LEFT, BELOW: The poolside palette at the Avalon Palm Springs recalls a glamorous Hollywood style. Cream cabanas are tipped in black, and bright yellow lounge chairs punctuate the space. Poolside furniture in the same hues will create a similar mood.

RIGHT: The vibrant patterns and bright colors of Moroccan carpets are on full display as they are used to create an innovative pool surround at the Peacock Pavilions in Marrakech. The carpets and a few colorful cushions and poufs transform a basic rectangular pool into an exotic and memorable outdoor retreat. This would be a fun idea to turn a poolside into a glamorous backdrop for a party.

Lounging

We all want to be more like our best vacation selves in real life—unhurried, worry-free, and mellow. So why not re-create a setting at home that led to a moment when you were completely relaxed? Start by recalling where you were during your favorite, most serene moments—the sleek daybed you lolled on for hours at a quiet beach, the afternoon spent poring over a new best-seller while swinging in a hammock, the wraparound sofa covered with pillows where you gathered with friends for cocktails. Bring an element of that into your own outdoor space—just having it available there will change your mindset, even if you don't get the chance to use it every day. Hang that embroidered hammock from Mexico up on the corner of your front porch. Set up that colorful hanging cocoon from the W in Vieques in your backyard. Take a cue from the Uxua Casa Hotel & Spa in Brazil and replace formal outdoor furniture from a catalog with floor cushions and low tables—a setup that will definitely inspire bare feet and lazy afternoons. You may not be able to be on permanent vacation, but this could be the next best thing.

PREVIOUS PAGES, LEFT: Woven wicker lampshades and chairs, purple-and-white fabric in a tropical print, and conch shells as décor all create an island vibe at the Cotton House on Mustique.

PREVIOUS PAGES, RIGHT: The sun shining through a woven canopy at La Sultana in Marrakech creates a rich tapestry of enchanting pattern that could be re-created as a reading nook on any sunny porch.

THIS PAGE: Sixty Hotels owner Jason Pomeranc and designer Carolina Eguiguren gave the lawn at the Nautilus in Miami a groovy spirit with a "lawn pod." The Shade Outdoor Daybed from Home Infatuation is customized here with tie-dye pillows and faux-fur blankets.

OPPOSITE, TOP: French designers Daniel Pouzet and Fred Frety were inspired by the concept of a bird's nest as a secluded sanctuary when they created their hanging Nestrest. It provides a beckoning, shaded oasis on Dedon Island in the Philippines. Any similar suspended pod would create an opportunity for a fun retreat.

OPPOSITE, BOTTOM: The hanging Cocoon chair designed by Patricia Urquiola for Moroso offers a cozy, vibrant, technicolor perch that instantly conjures up tropical escapes like the W Vieques.

OPPOSITE, TOP: A wide lawn is set up for fun at the Field Guide in Vermont thanks to a simple firepit, a few Acapulco chairs, and a shaded lounge area.

OPPOSITE, BOTTOM: Furniture that is low to the ground gives off a relaxed, unfussy vibe. At the Uxua Casa Hotel & Spa in Brazil, low tables, long cushions, and woven mats furnish a mellow, shaded outdoor lounge area. A similar nook could be created in a home yard, and an all-white scheme would inject it with a beachside serenity.

Above: The open-air library at the Azúcar illustrates how one sculptural, unique piece of furniture can define a space, and how one pop of color can make a small area interesting. If a pool house is in the plans at home, consider covering it with a grass roof for a memorably Caribbean note.

Nothing quite says "global flair" like a collection of fabrics from far-flung corners of the world. At the El Fenn in Morocco, striped local textiles and pillows in vivid hues liven up a rooftop seating area.

TOP: This cozy and cool lounge area at Dedon Island in the Philippines will inspire you to bring back the sunken living room craze of the 1970s. Wraparound sofas stacked with pillows made from local fabrics create an amazing setting for parties.

ABOVE: This soothing cream-and-white hut at the Lamai Serengeti in Tanzania is designed for relaxing. Re-creating a few key details at home, like the daybed piled high with pillows, the linen upholstery, or even just the calm palette, could make any porch or terrace exude the same sense of calm and quiet.

Jason Nixon and John Loecke

FOUNDERS OF MADCAP COTTAGE

Favorite Hotel: Taj Lake Palace, Udaipur, India

India's glorious Lake Pichola will transport you to a delightful dreamland. The former home of the local maharajah, the palace pairs a glorious history with stunning architecture—turrets, buttresses, and arches. Step off the private launch and you are showered with rose petals from unseen hands high above. The entire experience is magical. You can wander through a verdant courtyard filled with fountains and musicians like the resident flautist, dine high atop the lake on a terrace lit by flaming torches, or let yourself be transported in the colorful, lake-facing rooms that are the perfect mix of lavish and refined. And there's a cosseting service.

Best Part of the Overall Design

The hotel has an authenticity that is lacking at other luxury hotels that sit on Lake Pichola's far-off shore. This is the real thing—a true palace, not some Dubai-or-Disney-confection that oozes artifice and costume. This was a former working home, and you feel like you have been whisked away to the chicest of friends' royal palaces, if, indeed, you have such plucky pals. The setting was like nothing anywhere else in the world. How often can you say that an experience is 100 percent, hands-down unique?

Best Parts of the Room

Our room was the former domain of the maharani, the lady of the house, and was massive and overflowing with delicious details: John and I sprawled on the bed that hung from the ceiling on dangling chains, read glossy shelter magazines as we gazed onto the lake through colored-glass windows, and splashed around in the stone-clad bathroom like terry-clad devotees at an Elizabeth Arden day of beauty.

Most Unexpected Design Element

The details at the Taj Lake Palace are exceptional. No "moment" has been overlooked—from the lighting to the hardware to the fabric on a chair. The quality was exceptional. Bespoke brilliance rules the roost at the Taj Lake Palace.

Design Inspiration Brought Home

Take a white room, and layer it in rich blues, patchwork hues, and bold patterns. The stark white serves as the perfect launching pad for a dash of whimsy and will take a space from ho hum to "Hello, gorgeous!"

Photography Credits

Courtesy Ace Hotels: 14, 93, 97 top, 187, 217 bottom

Courtesy Altapura/L. Di Orio: 220 bottom

Courtesy Aman: 46 bottom, 56–57, 112 top, 112 bottom, 142, 154, 164, 166

Courtesy Auberge du Soleil: 141

Courtesy Avalon Palm Springs: 280

Courtesy Babylonstoren: 58, 161

Marco Badalian, courtesy Casa Tortugas: 259 bottom

Antoine Baralhé: 26, 207 top, 265

Bruno Barbosa, courtesy Vidago Palace: 243 bottom

Courtesy The Battery: 98 top, 99 top, 99 center right, 99 bottom right

John Bedell, courtesy The Battery: 99 bottom left

Jane Beiles for The Chequit: 43 top, 134

Linda Berman, courtesy Nihiwatu Puncak: 278

Courtesy Blancaneaux Lodge/Family Coppola Resorts: 20

Courtesy Michele Bonan: 252 top right

Ken Bound, courtesy Locanda al Colle: 236 bottom right

Paul Bowyer: 81, 96 bottom, 147 top, 147 bottom, 206 bottom, 220 top left

Courtesy Alessandra Branca: 175 top left

Courtesy The Brice: 125, 183 bottom, 216 bottom

Simon Brown, courtesy Firmdale Hotels: 2–3, 27, 104, 123 top, 198, 205 top, 216

Bruce Buck: 223 bottom

Bruce Buck, courtesy St. Regis: 249 top

Courtesy The Carlyle, A Rosewood Hotel: 252 bottom

Courtesy Casa Laguna: 123 bottom

Courtesy Casa Tortugas/Holbox Hotels: 66

Courtesy Casas del XVI: 37, 49 bottom, 87, 119

Courtesy Claridge's/Maybourne Hotel Group: 253 top, 253 bottom

Courtesy The Chequit: 236 bottom

Courtesy Colony Palms: 84, 269 bottom

Courtesy Condesa DF: 65

Courtesy The Confidante: 280

Courtesy The Connaught/Maybourne Hotel Group: 86

Courtesy Continentale Hotel/Lungarno Collection: 249 bottom

Courtesy C.O.Q.: 12 top, 161 top right, 236 top

Courtesy Cotton House Resort Mustique: 282

Courtesy Dar Seven: 47, 48

Kip Dawkins, courtesy Quirk Hotel: 180

Courtesy Dedon Island: 155 top, 285 top, 289 top

Courtesy Ett Hem: 10, 68, 90, 100–101, 106, 138, 261

De Simone Design, Sydney: 242

Serge Detalle: 38–39

Nicolas Dumont: 76 bottom, 184 bottom, 228–9, 274 top

George Fakaros, courtesy Mystique/Starwood: 169 bottom

Floto + Warner: 78–79, 92 top

Courtesy Four Seasons Hotels: 25 bottom, 279

Adrian Gaut for SIXTY Hotels: 256, 284

Hervé Goluza: 81, 185 top, 193 bottom, 204, 222, 234 top, 260, 273

Courtesy Grace Bay Resorts: 108 top

Janos Grapow, courtesy Portrait Firenze/Lungarno Collection: 59

Sam Gray Photography, courtesy Edson Hill: 49, 119 top, 127 top

Courtesy The Greenwich Hotel: 11, 130–31

Courtesy Hotel Capo La Gala: 241 top, 241 bottom

Courtesy Hotel Covell: 162

Courtesy Hotel Dylan: 202–3

Courtesy Hotel Emma: 139

Courtesy Hotel Escondido/Grupohabita: 184

Courtesy Hotel Fabric: 200 bottom

Courtesy Hotel Jerome/Auberge Resorts: 103, 117, 225 bottom

Courtesy Hotel Providence: 250

Courtesy Hotel Recamier: 16, 17

Courtesy Hoxton Hotels: 12 bottom, 77 bottom, 95 bottom, 96 top, 153 bottom, 206 top, 214, 215, 237 top, 237 bottom right, 239, 264

Courtesy The Imperial, New Delhi: 128 top, 128 center, 128 bottom, 129 top, 129 center, 129 bottom left, 129 bottom right

Courtesy J.K. Places: 72 bottom, 82, 109, 126 top, 170

Laure Joliet, courtesy The Buchanan, a Kimpton Hotel: 223 top, 250 top, 250 bottom

Andrea Jones, courtesy Borgo Santo Pietro: 274

Courtesy Kasbah Tamadot/Virgin: 61 top left, 61 top right

Nikolas Koenig: 199 bottom

Jaime Kowal: 21 top

Courtesy Kurland Hotel: 190

Courtesy La Mamounia: 52, 115, 244, 267

Courtesy La Minervetta: 94, 145 top, 145 bottom, 153 top, 178, 179

Courtesy La Reserve: 174 top, 174 bottom, 175 top right, 175 center, 175 bottom

Courtesy La Sultana: 53, 238, 283

Acknowledgments

Thank you to everyone who made this book possible, starting with the over three hundred hotels that shared images of their stunning properties. A million thanks to the best agent a writer could ask for, Alison Fargis, who never gave up on this idea. Indebted to my editor Stacee Gravelle Lawrence, who shaped every aspect of Hotel Chic at Home. Kudos to Patricia Fabricant and Jena Sher for their beautiful vision and graphic designs.

Thank you so much to the brilliant designers who shared their favorite hotels and travel design inspiration—Mary McDonald, Alessandra Branca, John Robshaw, Joe Lucas, Suysel dePedro Cunningham and Anne Maxwell Foster, Christiane Lemieux, John Loecke, Jason Oliver Nixon, and Michele Bonan.

Finally and most important, thank you to my family—my parents, who ignited my love for hotels and design from an early age, my awesome siblings—and my absolute loves Brooks, Elliott, and Liv.

Published in the United States by The Monacelli Press
Library of Congress Control Number: 2016942383
ISBN: 978-1-58093-475-6
Printed in China
Designed by Patricia Fabricant
1 3 5 7 9 10 8 6 4 2
First Edition

The Monacelli Press
236 West 27th Street
New York, New York 10001

www.monacellipress.com